Essentials of

ADVERTISING STRATEGY

By DON E. SCHULTZ

Essentials of
ADVERTISING STRATEGY

By DON E. SCHULTZ

Crain Books
740 Rush Street
Chicago, IL 60611

Contents

Dedication

To the people most responsible for the development of the concepts and principles of creative strategy described in this book, particularly:

- Dr. John E. Mertes, who, in the 1950s at the University of Oklahoma, was teaching these same concepts and principles but with different words.
- Morris L. Hite, who in the 1960s, was practicing and applying these same principles and concepts for clients of Tracy-Locke with spectacular results.
- Larry L. Pontius, who in the 1970s, demonstrated how these ideas and principles could be put into a form students could understand and use.

These three may never have met except through me and through the pages of this book. To them and the many others from whom I have learned, this book is dedicated.

Foreword

Well after the manuscript for this book was completed, a former student sent me the article below, written by Nancy Sutton, Grey Advertising — New York. It summed up my own feelings about creative strategy so well that I asked permission to reprint it as an introductory piece to this text.[1]

Nancy's comments reflect my own feelings about creative strategy. You'll see that as you go through the text. Unfortunately, though, there still are creative people who resist the discipline of a strategy. Somehow, they seem to feel it inhibits their creativity or their God-given right to do whatever they wish. There still may be places for these creative mavericks, but there aren't many in today's results-oriented marketplace.

For major marketers and advertising agencies, creative strategies are a way of life. If you plan to succeed in advertising, Nancy's advice on how to live with and profit from a strategy will be invaluable. As she so aptly puts it, "The strategy is not a drag. It is power. Use it."

Thanks, Nancy. I hope after reading this book all creative people will "Get to the Point."

Get to the Point

By Nancy Sutton

AND THE POINT IS NOT your mortgage. Never be a coward.

And the point is not your reel. Never be a fool.

The point, friend, when you sit down to create a piece of advertising is The Strategy. Get to it.

Let lesser minds tinker around with Burke openings and borrowed interest. You get to work on the strategy.

A lot of neatly pressed people with expensive educations have labored hard to produce that piece of paper. It may look arid to you. Arid. Uninspiring. Uninteresting. Boring. And, yes, familiar: "hello there women 25-64 with some high school education, working and non-working, with household incomes of $10M plus."

But to the neatly pressed, that piece of paper is insightful, incisive, disciplined, precise, brilliant, even masterful.

Furthermore, you're stuck with it.

Brilliant advertising that isn't on strategy is not brilliant advertising, and you're not going to sell it. Remember the scenario? First they look at the strategy. Then they look at the advertising.

If that piece of paper that's been nitpicked and struggled over and formally agreed to says "convenient," you must deliver convenience.

If it says "safer," you must deliver safety.

Convenient. Safer. Cleaner. Brighter. Whiter. Easier. Juicier. Faster. New. New. New. This is sacred vocabulary to the neatly pressed. Don't feel superior to it. Don't be bored by it. Don't ignore it.

Don't try to rise above the strategy. Instead, come to grips with it. Get inside it. And deliver it. Deliver it with shining dazzle: that's your job, and that's your power.

The words on that piece of paper are the straight and narrow path — God knows straight, and God knows narrow — to selling an exciting advertising idea. If the critical words are there, your execution can light up the skies. If the critical words are there, you can get brilliant conceptual thinking through all those nervous Nellies on the junior levels of both the agency and the client. They may be terrified of it because it is fresh and innovative, but if it's on strategy — absolutely on strategy — you can keep it alive and get it up the line to someone who has creative taste and creative courage.

The strategy is not a drag. It is power. Use it.

In a long and lovely career at Grey, my favorite commercial is "Big Bowl" for Post Raisin Bran: twelve fat men dressed up like raisins in floppy hats and brown velvet suits hamming it up outrageously in a ten-foot bowl filled with gigantic papier-mache flakes. It is a singing commercial — a zany, happy, nutty singing commercial. The lyrics are:

It's raisins that make Post Raisin Bran so wonderful.
It's raisins that make Post Raisin Bran so different.
It's raisins that make Post Raisin Bran so raisin-y.
More raisins.
Lots more raisins.
More raisins than any other Raisin Bran.
If you like raisins, fat juicy raisins, you'll like Post Raisin Bran more.

Sure, I'm a creative genius.

Sure, it was finished on the second draft.

I won a lot of prizes as the writer. Not fair. The lyrics are simply the strategy statements. The real writers were a bunch of MBAs in neatly pressed suits.

More raisins. That's right in there with Convenient. Safer. Cleaner. Brighter. Whiter. Easier. Juicier. Faster. New. New. New. All those weary words in all those strategy statements.

Don't rise above them. Get inside them. And make them sing.

The term "a writer's writer" is often overused. But somehow, when a piece of copy just doesn't sing, someone will always suggest, "Maybe Nancy should take a crack at it." Vice President/Group Creative Director NANCY SUTTON is in her eighteenth year at Grey-New York.

Note

1. "Get to the Point" by Nancy Sutton originally appeared in Grey View, a publication of Grey Advertising, Inc. It is reprinted with the permission of Grey Advertising Inc. ©Grey Advertising Inc. 1980.

Introduction

WOMAN #2: Charmin's so squeezably soft, it's irresistible.

WHIPPLE: Please don't squeeze the Charmin!

Hoffmeier, in my store nobody squeezes the Charmin!

WHIPPLE: Ohh ...

ANNCR: (VO) Charmin. So big and fluffy, so squeezably soft ...

WHIPPLE: it's irresistible.

FIGURE I-1 Mr. Whipple has been speaking for Charmin tissue for more than 10 years. A recent study by Bruskin Research found that more than 80 per cent of the people interviewed correctly identified the "Please don't squeeze the Charmin" slogan.

Why is it some of the ads you enjoy the most appear only once or twice and then disappear forever while Mr. Whipple goes on selling the softness of Charmin bathroom tissue year after year? What about Madge the Manicurist? Is she a sound way to convince women Palmolive dishwashing liquid will make their hands soft? Is the "Veg-O-Matic" salesman with his mile-a-minute delivery the best creative approach for a vegetable slicer, grater, peeler, etc.? Why did the cute Alka-Seltzer commercials, such as "Spicy Meatballs" and the "Young Bride" who made the dumpling, disappear from television?

In short, why is it the advertisements that win the "creative" awards often don't win at the cash register? The purpose of this text, is to help you answer that question by increasing your understanding of what makes good advertising and by helping you determine what makes good **creative** advertisements or commercials.

What This Book Is and What It Isn't

Because the terms *creative* and *creativity* have been overused and misused in advertising, it's important to clarify immediately what this text is and what it isn't.

First, it's a text on the basics of advertising strategy, the broad all-encom-

You're soaking in it.

WOMAN: Dishwashing liquid? (LAUGHTER)
MADGE: It's Palmolive.

WOMAN: Mild?

Makes heaps of suds that last. And like I said, Palmolive softens hands while you do the dishes.

WOMAN: Madge, I'm cuckoo over Palmolive. (SFX: CLOCK)

MADGE: That makes two of you. (LAUGHTER)

FIGURE I-2. Madge the Manicurist has been the spokesperson for Palmolive dishwashing liquid for more than 12 years. The advertising has helped Palmolive grow from a very minor share to the second leading dishwashing brand in the country.

passing ideas of advertising. It's not a text on copywriting, art direction, layout, etc. You may learn the rudiments of those subjects from this book but not the specific skills.

Second, our purpose is to help you understand advertising, advertising messages, and advertising executions. You will learn how to separate the good from the bad. To do this we'll look at the broad areas of creative advertising, not the specifics — although you'll find plenty of examples to illustrate the points.

Third, we'll use something which is often anathema to creative people — the checklist. It will help you remember and understand the subject better. That is, it will help in learning, not necessarily in doing.

Finally, there will probably be parts of this book with which you won't agree. That's to be expected. All evaluations of advertising are subjective. What appeals to you may not appeal to me, and what appeals to both of us might not influence the target market for our message. The secret of understanding advertising creativity is to try to remove your personal feelings from your judgment. Try to see what your customer or prospect will like and respond to, not what you care for. That's a key point we'll keep coming back to over and over; see advertising from your prospect's view, not your own.

With those general ground rules, we are ready to start.

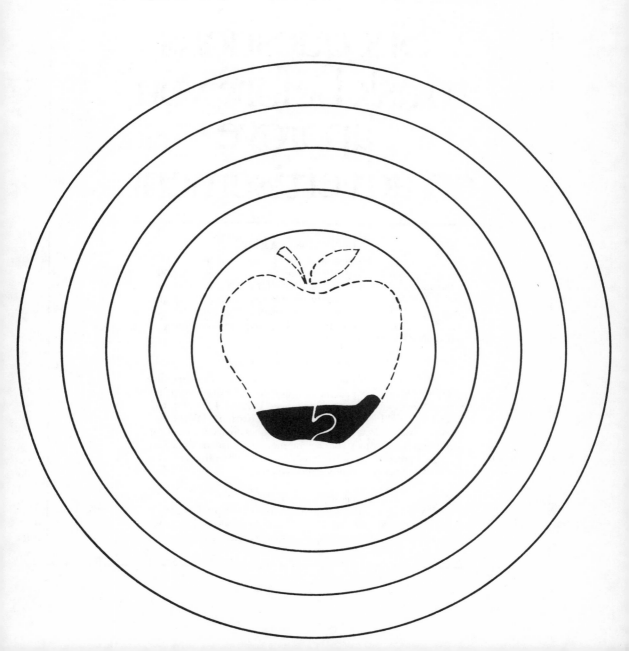

What *is* "creative advertising"? That question may have been best answered by an advertisement used by one of this country's largest advertising agencies, Benton & Bowles, when they said "It's not creative unless it sells." Read the ad carefully. It's full of advertising truths, truths we'll be discussing in more detail on the following pages.

To illustrate the point a bit more, here's a simple test you can take.

1. Did you watch television last night?
    ☐ Yes
    ☐ No
    (If you checked no, wait until a day on which you can answer yes)

Six questions to ask before you approve an advertisement.

1. Is there a big idea?

Nothing else is so important to the success of an advertisement. A genuine selling idea transcends execution. Before you approve any advertisement, ask yourself if it really has a big idea and if that idea emerges clearly, emphatically, and single-mindedly. Ask yourself: Is it an *important* idea—such as Scope's "medicine breath," the positioning of Pledge furniture polish as a dusting aid, or AMF's "We make weekends."

2. Is there a theme line?

A theme line that presents your selling idea in a memorable set of words can be worth millions of dollars of extra mileage to your advertising. Provocative lines like "When E.F. Hutton talks, people listen," "Please don't squeeze the Charmin," "We really move our tail for you" (Continental Airlines) make it easy for the customer to remember your selling message. Incidentally, when you get a great one, treasure it and use it prominently in every print ad and television commercial you run.

3. Is it relevant?

If your advertising is remembered but your product forgotten, you might as well run "compliments of a friend." Jokes that steal attention from the selling idea, inappropriate entertainment

FIGURE 1-1

2. How long did you watch?
   ☐ One hour
   ☐ Two hours
   ☐ Three hours
   ☐ More
3. Name one commercial you remember seeing:

   What was the product category? _____

   What was the brand? _____

   What was the main selling idea? _____

---

devices, celebrities who have no logical connection with your product, and other irrelevancies can be devastating. Look for relevance in every advertising execution.

4. Is it hackneyed?

Is the advertisement fresh, innovative, and original or is it merely a pale carbon copy of somebody *else's* advertising? Too much advertising is look-alike, sound-alike advertising. These advertisements are often costly failures. Don't run the risk of being mistaken for your competitor. Demand an execution that is all your own.

5. Does it demonstrate?

Nothing works harder or sells better than a demonstration of your product's superiority, especially in television. Look for every opportunity to demonstrate. If you can't demonstrate, at least show the product in use. Demonstrations—such as the simple exposition of how the Trac II razor works or the coating action of Pepto-Bismol—are convincing ways to sell.

6. Is it believable?

Does the advertising overpromise? Does the selling idea sound a false note? An advertisement can be totally truthful, yet sound unbelievable. Better to underpromise and be believable than to overpromise and lose credibility.

We know that great advertising is not made by rules nor created by guidelines. It comes from creative people. However, we also know from experience that most successful advertising has certain readily identifiable and wholly predictable qualities. We have listed six. There are others. We would like nothing better than to show you some of the advertising that illustrates these points.

Please call or write Jack Bowen, President, Benton & Bowles, Inc., 909 Third Avenue, New York, N.Y. 10022. Telephone: (212) 758-6200.

Benton&Bowles

New York, Chicago, Los Angeles, and other major cities worldwide.

It's not creative unless it sells.

7

If you're an average American and watched at least one hour of television the previous night, you probably remember only one commercial, if you remember any at all. During that hour, you were probably exposed to more than 25 30-second commercials, plus numerous station plugs, upcoming show announcements, etc. Yet, you may recall only one, or at the most two, commercials.

Research has shown that most people recall only about one out of every 14 commercials they are exposed to. Why? What makes one commercial memorable while others are not? What makes one advertisement or commercial stand out in your mind?

It's usually the creative product. It's the message of the advertisement or the way the advertising is presented. That's what separates successful from unsuccessful advertising. It's what sends people out into the streets looking for a specific brand. It's what makes a common, everyday product into a "best seller."

But Isn't All Advertising Creative?

In the loosest sense of the word, yes, all advertising is creative. It's creative because it's a creation — someone had to sit down and think up a message and a way to present it through a media form. But, no, not all advertising is *creative* because *creative* means "to bring into existence out of nothing, to originate, to make."

When we talk about a product that has a specific consumer benefit or solves a consumer problem, we really aren't "bringing something into existence out of nothing"; we may be merely communicating the product benefit in a memorable form or at least in a way that appeals to the prospect or consumer. In most cases, it's the product that has the creativity for the consumer. The advertising is simply taking an effective form to present the benefit.

The key point to remember is that if there is nothing of benefit to the consumer, if an advertisement or a commercial is developed out of thin air, that is true "creative advertising." We've made something out of nothing. Unfortunately, most people don't purchase products because of the "creativity" of the advertising. They buy products for the benefits they receive or the problems the product solves.

Some practitioners have called the development of effective selling messages *controlled creativity*. That means simply the creativity is in the presentation of the message, not in the consumer benefit of the product or the problem solved. That's an important point. We'll be discussing it in greater detail on the following pages. We'll also look at content versus execution and controlled versus uncontrolled creativity.

What's the Real Importance of Advertising Creativity?

When we get right down to it, advertising, in spite of all its glamor, its mystique, its excitement, is a very simple business. It consists only of getting the right message to the right audience at the right time. It is nothing more than that. But it is nothing less. The problem is that there are literally hundreds, if not thousands, of advertisers who are trying to do the same thing at the same time with the same audience through the same channels. That's where the need for a creative advertising product comes in.

Let's face it. Not many consumers are really all that interested in advertising. How many times have you heard someone say, "Let's sit down and watch a few commercials on television" or "Let's pick up a copy of *Time* and look at the ads" or "I can hardly wait to get the *Sunday New York Times* so I can see all the interesting Macy advertisements"? Probably not often.

But advertising *does* play an important part in people's lives. It also plays an important part in the success or failure of many businesses.

Getting the right message to the right audience at the right time is not an easy job. Recent studies have proported to show the "average person" in the United States sees 35 television commercials, hears 38 radio spots, sees 15 magazine ads, 185 newspaper ads, and 12 outdoor messages *every day of every week*. All told, if you're an average American adult, you'll be assaulted by a minimum of 560 advertising messages daily. Some estimates go as high as 1,600.

When you consider that this bombardment never stops, the true value of creativity in advertising becomes obvious. It takes an extremely provocative approach to get a message through to anyone. The message that gets through the "information clutter" and "advertising noise" surrounding the consumer has exhibited true advertising creativity.

We'll come back to creativity in advertising many times in this text. Remember, though, creative advertising is not manufacturing something from nothing. It is the ability to take a product benefit or a solution to a consumer problem and present it in an effective and memorable way. In most cases, the key advertising decision is "what to say," not "how to say it." That's what this book is really about. It will show you how to determine the best thing to say. How to say it comes in the actual practice of copywriting, layout, etc.

The Checkpoint Approach

If you're a beginner in advertising, your experience is probably more in the area of advertising consumption than advertising development. For that reason, this text leans heavily on a series of checkpoints or lists.

Even if you've never written an ad or commercial, you've probably heard "experts and authorities" decry the use of such crutches. We use them here for a purpose. When you are learning, you need a guide. The checkpoint is a form of guide. As you become more skilled, the lists will come naturally. You'll review the suggested checkpoints of advertisements or commercials automatically. The checkpoint is simply a way to make sure you've not left anything out or missed any important point. Even David Ogilvy, one of the recognized geniuses in the advertising field, uses the checkpoint approach. Read his book *"Confessions of an Advertising Man."* You'll find list after list of ideas and suggestions such as "The nine best ads I ever wrote."

Some Necessary Definitions

Before proceeding, let's take a look at some important definitions. Terminology in advertising, particularly in the creative area, has a way of meaning different things to different people. So there will be no misunderstanding, here's what we mean when we talk about:

Advertising Objective: A clearly stated, measurable end result of an advertising message or messages. Usually the objective is measured in terms of a change in awareness, preference, conviction or other communication effect.

↓

Creative Strategy or Advertising Strategy: The formulation of an advertising message that communicates the benefit or problem solution characteristics of the product or service to the target market. It is generally developed for use in the mass media.

↓

Advertising Execution: The physical form in terms of art, illustration, copy, music, etc., in which the advertising strategy is presented to the target market to achieve the advertising objective(s).

Having established these definitions, we can be a bit more descriptive about what this text will cover. We will be primarily interested in how to develop creative or advertising strategies to fulfill the advertising objectives. We will not focus on advertising executions, although Chapter 5, 7 and 8 give some general guidelines. Because an advertising strategy can be executed in literally hundreds of ways, primary emphasis will be on "what to say" rather than "how to say it." Strategy is the message we want to deliver. The execution is the way it is said or the way it is presented. Strategy is always the overriding theme. All executions must be checked back against the strategy to make sure they fit. If they don't, the execution is the culprit, not the strategy. You can't have effective advertising without a sound advertising strategy no matter how "creative" you may be.

Chapter 2
How Advertising Works

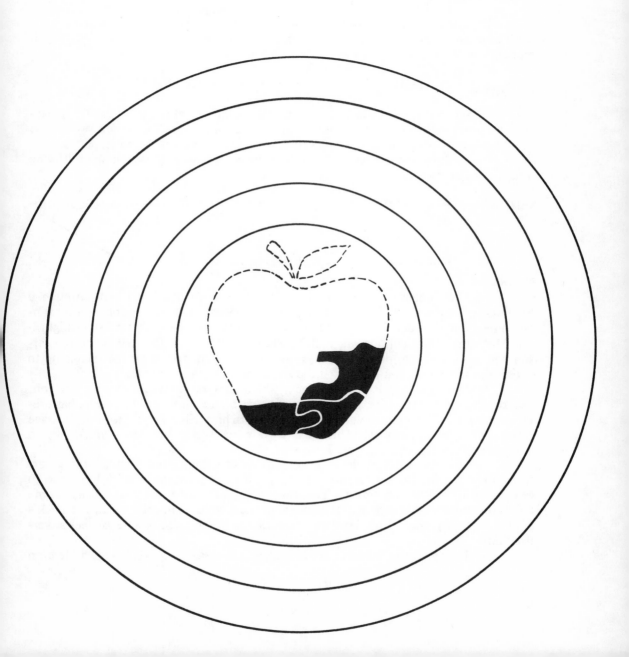

Essentials of Advertising Strategy

Today's American economy is built primarily on mass—mass production, mass consumption, mass purchasing, and, in many cases, mass media. Advertising has been a major factor in building this economic system. If manufacturers had no way to communicate the advantages of their products and services to large audiences or were still dependent on consumers searching for particular products, America's spectacular growth might never have occurred.

We can almost draw a direct correlation between the growth of mass production in America and the development of mass communication. These two systems have become so intertwined it is difficult to determine which aided which the most. Regardless of the order, modern merchandisers depend on mass communication to get their advertising messages to consumers.

How Does Communication Work?

To understand advertising, we must first understand mass communication. The basic model for the communication process was developed from Ivan Pavlov's work with dogs. His concept was that a stimulus will result in a response. Called the S-R model, it is illustrated in this way:

STIMULUS ⟶ RESPONSE

FIGURE 2-1

When this model is applied to human communication, the same thing happens. In other words, if a stimulus in the form of a communication occurs, a response should result. If no communication occurs, obviously there will be no response.

By applying the basic S-R model to the communication system the following model was developed:

FIGURE 2-2

The Sender develops a Message which is encoded and sent through a Medium to the Receiver. For example, assume you want to invite a friend over for dinner. You are the Sender. The Message is "Come to my house for dinner Friday night." The Medium is the telephone with which you call the Receiver. The Receiver is the person you are inviting to dinner. Thus, when you call your friend on the telephone to invite him to dinner, you have used the basic communication model.

The final step is the Feedback, which lets you know whether or not your friend received the Message. In this case, if he agrees to come or tells you he has previous plans, you know you have communicated with him. His response to your Message is your indication of Feedback. This is exactly how mass communication works, only on a much larger scale with multiple Receivers.

To convert this model to an advertising situation, assume you are the advertising manager for Blick's Department Store. You're planning a week-long sale to celebrate Blick's 50th anniversary. You want people to know about your sale and come to it, so you develop a message. Assume your message is "Gigantic savings at Blick's 50th anniversary sale." You develop your message in the form of a newspaper advertisement.

Thus you, the Sender, have developed a Message to send through a Medium

14

to your Receivers, all of whom are customers and prospects in your sales area. You will learn if your Message was received by the Feedback of your Receivers. In this case, if more people than normal come to Blick's for the 50th anniversary sale, you assume they received your Message.

This simple communications model was subscribed to until the late 1940s. It was called the "hypodermic effect" of communications because it was similar to a hypodermic syringe. It was believed that the more messages "shot" into the target, the greater the response. In fact, some people feared the public could be manipulated simply by using massive numbers of messages that would totally overwhelm people and make them do almost anything.

After a number of experiments, people showed they were not nearly as helpless in the communications process as was thought. Studies proved that people had the ability to filter or screen out unwanted or useless messages. Based on the work of communications experts such as Professors Paul Lazarfeld, C.I. Hoveland, Wilbur Schramm, and others, a new mass communications model was developed:

FIGURE 2-3

According to this model, the Sender may develop an excellent Message and place it in the proper Medium where the Receiver is exposed to it, but the Receiver may choose to block or filter the Message rather than receive it. In other words, all systems are GO until the Message reaches the Receiver. It is then that the Receiver determines whether or not to actually receive the Message.[1]

In addition, other factors occur in the communications process in the form of Noise or interference in the communication of the message. The model below illustrates where noise (illustrated by the SS figures) might occur.

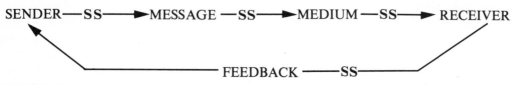

FIGURE 2-4

In this case, Noise could occur in any one or all of several places in the model. For example, the Sender might develop a poor Message. The wording might not be correct or the language not be proper. Thus, Noise occurs in the link between the Sender and the Message. Noise also can occur between the Message and the Medium. This could be the improper handling of the Message. Perhaps the words got scrambled or the pictures were upside down or backward. In addition, Noise can occur between the Medium and the Receiver. This could be the result of conflicting messages, clutter from other messages or lack of proper orientation. Noise also can occur between the Receiver and the Sender in the Feedback loop. The Receiver might get the Message but not react in an anticipated way.

Once again, let's use the example of Blick's Department Store's 50th anniversary sale. Noise can occur because you, the advertising manager, didn't write a very good Message for the 50th anniversary sale. People may not believe the values are very exciting or that you really want them to come. Noise also can occur between the Message and the Medium. For example, you may have had ladies dresses, priced originally at $39.95, on sale for $14.95. In placing your Message, the sale price was incorrectly given as $34.95, certainly not the big saving you had in mind. Similarly, Noise may be present between the Medium and the Receiver. There may be other sales advertised which your prospects regard as better values or they may see but not read your advertisement in the newspaper that day.

Noise may occur even in the Feedback loop. For example, the Message may have been received and the Receiver planned to go to the sale but the car wouldn't run or a sudden emergency made it impossible. As you can see, the model becomes quite complex when all the possibilities are considered. Nevertheless, the actual advertising communication model is even more complex.

From these illustrations, it is apparent that advertising is a form of communication and, in our modern society, it is usually a form of *mass* communication. To differentiate advertising from other forms of mass communication, we define advertising as the communication of a sales message or a persuasive message designed to influence the opinions or actions of persons in favor of the advertised brand. Other forms of mass communication may not have this persuasive nature or seek to influence the actions of the receiver.

First, A Look at Buyer Behavior

To understand how advertising works, we must first look at how buyers operate in the marketplace.

Unfortunately, as in so many areas in which we seek to understand human behavior, our knowledge of how the individual buyer operates is quite limited. As a result, researchers have suggested several models of buyer behavior. Some have received more support than others, but there is still no single accepted model to turn to for an explanation.

Generally four theory groups or models of buyer or consumer behavior have been developed:

1. **Psychological Models.** All these models suggest buyers mentally respond in some way to external stimuli or the environment. For example, the mass communications model described previously is a psychological model of how we believe communication works.

2. **Economic Models.** In these models, all persons are considered rational creatures. Based on the market, the price and other considerations, a person supposedly makes a logical and rational choice in each buying decision. For example, one economic model of buyer behavior suggests that all persons seek pleasure and avoid pain. Thus, they will use their income to purchase the most pleasure they can or to avoid the worst pain or unpleasantness. All buying decisions, therefore, are based on increasing pleasure or avoiding pain. Other economic models suggest rational people know and understand the market and make logical choices after studying all alternatives.

3. **Sociological Models.** In these models, the forms, institutions,

and functions of social groups directly influence purchasing behavior. In other words, people make buying decisions based on their social status or perceived social position. In these models, buying behavior is explained by life style, reference groups, and the various social states.

4. **Statistical Models.** The statistical models make no attempt to explain buyer behavior. Instead, they attempt to group or identify past or present purchasers of products or services. In doing this, they make the assumption that all persons who fall into the identified groups are logical prospects for a product or service. Because children between the ages of 5 and 15 consume the most cold cereal, they are believed to comprise the best market for cold cereals. Other statistical models use similar approaches.[2]

All buyer behavior models have their supporters and one can make a case for each approach. It is exactly this confusion that has prevented a single model from being widely embraced by academicians and practitioners.

In spite of these problems in understanding the complete concept of how buyer behavior works, there is general agreement on how the buying process occurs among people in the market.

Understanding the Buying Process

Most information about the buying process is based on the adoption process model, often called the "Diffusion of Innovation" model, developed by Everett Rogers. Rogers was a communications specialist who was interested in how people learn about new ideas and new products. Much of his work was done among the native tribes of South America where new ideas such as sanitation, personal hygiene, and child care were virtually unknown. By bringing new ideas to the natives, Rogers was able to study how new ideas spread or "diffused" among the population.

He found that a new idea usually went through six separate steps:

Awareness of the new idea.

Interest in the new idea.

Evaluation of the new idea as to whether it offered value to the person.

Trial of the new idea.

Decision after trial as to whether or not the new idea was worthwhile.

Confirmation that the idea was worth continuing.[3]

Many experts have suggested that the buying process for a product or service occurs in the same way as the diffusion of any new idea. People become aware of the product, develop an interest in it, determine if there is sufficient reason to try or buy it, purchase the product for trial or use, make a decision as to whether or not the product is of sufficient value to continue use, and then continue using the product if satisfied. A very simple model of the buying process, called AIDA, was developed in the 1920s, and it follows the same pattern Rogers suggested in his diffusion model. The AIDA model looks like this:

Attention First the person must become aware of the product or service. This
  ↓   requires getting his attention.

Interest Simply being aware of the product does not make a sale. Consumer
  ↓   interest must be generated to separate this specific product from the
      multitude that exist.

Desire From interest, desire must grow. Usually desire grows out of the
  ↓   benefits the product offers or the solution it proposes for a problem
      the consumer has.

Action Once desire is built, the final step is action. The person desiring the
      product must take the final step to purchase it.

Other models of how the buying process is believed to work also have been developed. Most follow this somewhat simplistic approach. As we previously discussed, there is some question as to whether or not an accurate outline of the buying process can be developed in the modern marketplace.

Some researchers have suggested that purchasing decisions often may be made simply on impulse without a specific series of steps. In these cases, the same buying decision may occur but all the steps in the process may take only an instant as a person is standing in front of a cashier and purchasing an unknown brand of gum or candy. We have made great strides in understanding human behavior, but there is still much to learn, particularly in the area of buyer behavior and the buying process.

While we may not know everything about buyer behavior or the buying process, there is sufficient evidence of certain activities so that we may make some generalized statements. We know most consumers mentally determine that they will or won't purchase a product. Whether this is determined by psychological, economic, or sociological reasons, it does occur. Next, we know that there is probably some sort of buying process through which consumers move as they decide whether or not to purchase a product. Whether this process is a series of steps such as AIDA or the more compressed version of impulse purchase, there is little doubt that a mental process is involved.

How We Believe Advertising Works

With the preceeding brief description of the communication process, buyer behavior, and the buying process, can we relate this to a logical advertising model? The answer is yes, *maybe*. Figure 2-5 describes what we believe happens in the communication of an advertising message, up to a point. [4]

Advertising has multiple Senders with Messages attempting to reach the same Receiver. Advertising Messages are sent through the advertising Medium where they are Screened by the Receiver. Noise occurs all along the way.

Assuming the Receiver does not Screen out the Message, one of two things will happen when the Message is decoded. It either elicits a direct response or it is "stored" for future use. This storage mechanism is an important part of the advertising model because it is the basis by which most advertising is evaluated. We will discuss it in detail later.

As you can see, this advertising model looks much like the standard communications model we described previously. There are, however, a number of questions and problems in determining if this is exactly how advertising really works. For example, Dr. Herbert Krugman of General Electric has suggested that under certain

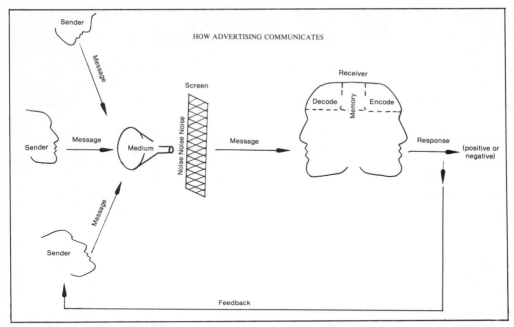

FIGURE 2-5

situations, such as watching television, learning or receiving advertising messages may occur without the Receiver paying specific attention. In other words, there is learning without involvement. Because the television viewer is in a relaxed state, the Receiver may not use his Screening device or may not "mediate" the Messages. Thus, advertising Messages may go directly into "storage" for use at a later date, perhaps even unconsciously.[5]

Another suggestion is that with the low cost of many products and the increase in impulse purchases by consumers, advertising may not even have an effect until after purchase. In other words, the purchase or use of a product is the "trigger" which activates the acceptance of an advertising message. The Receiver may not even be aware of Messages until after the product has been used. These are just two of the problems related to how advertising works.

Even if we can't explain all the steps, most people agree advertising *does* work. In an effort to explain the advertising process in a more logical sequence, Robert Lavidge and Gary Steiner developed an approach that seems to tie all the previous models into one package. It is called the "Hierarchy of Effects" model.

Specifically, Lavidge and Steiner suggest:

"Advertising may be thought of as a force which must move people up a series of steps:

1. Near the bottom of the steps stand the potential purchasers who are completely unaware of the existence of the product or service in question.

2. Closer to purchasing, but still a long way from the cash register, are those who are merely aware of its existence.

3. Up a step are prospects who know what the product has to offer.

LAVIDGE & STEINER MODEL HIERARCHY OF EFFECTS

Lavidge & Steiner Model Hierarchy of Effects

Related Behavioral Dimensions	Movement toward purchase	Examples of types of promotion or advertising relevant to various steps
CONATIVE the realm of motives. Ads stimulate or direct desires.	PURCHASE	Point-of-purchase Retail store ads Deals "Last chance" offers Price appeals Testimonials
	CONVICTION	
AFFECTIVE the realm of emotions. Ads change attitudes and feelings.	PREFERENCE	Competitive ads Argumentative copy "Image" ads Status, glamour appeals
	LIKING	
COGNITIVE the realm of thoughts. Ads provide information and facts.	KNOWLEDGE	Announcements Descriptive copy Classified ads Slogans Jingles Sky writing Teaser campaigns
	AWARENESS	

FIGURE 2-6 Steiner/Lavidge Model

4. Still closer to purchasing are those who have favorable attitudes toward the product — those who like the product.

5. Those whose favorable attitudes have developed to the point of preference over all other possibilities are up still another step.

6. Even closer to purchasing are consumers who couple preference with a desire to buy and the conviction that the purchase would be wise.

7. Finally, of course, is the step which translates this attitude into an actual purchase."[6]

The Lavidge and Steiner approach is primarily a psychological model of buyer behavior that has been related to the standard communications model. With some exceptions, the Lavidge and Steiner model is accepted as the definition of how advertising works.

The Lavidge and Steiner model is important for another reason. It offers a method of evaluating the effects of advertising. By measuring changes or movement up the "Hierarchy of Effects," we are often able to determine what effects advertising is having. That's an important point. Advertisers want to know if their advertising is working and that's why most of them now use some form of the Lavidge and Steiner model to evaluate advertising effectiveness.

Chapter 3
Marketing, Advertising, And Sales

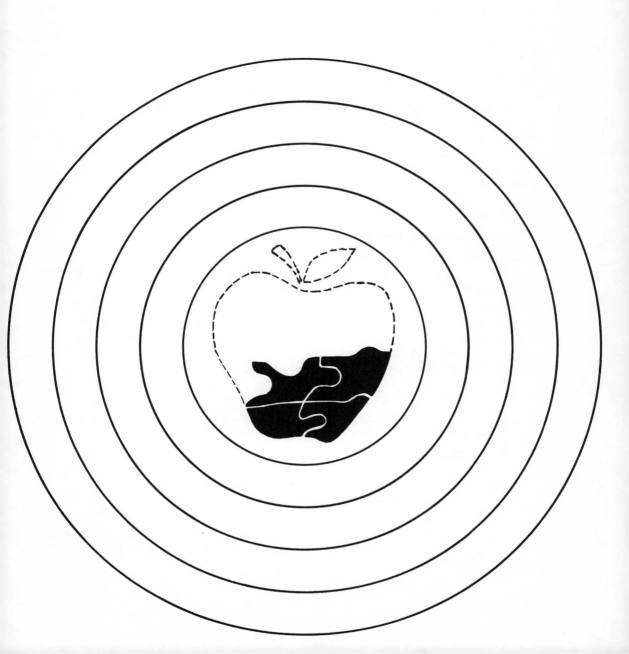

To this point, we've discussed advertising from what may appear to be only a theoretical view. That is, we've described how we think mass communication operates and how advertising works or affects people. From this discussion, it may seem advertising is the major ingredient in the selling of a product or service. But while advertising may be important, it usually is just one of many ingredients in the marketing mix. To fully understand advertising, we must comprehend how modern marketing-oriented organizations function.

The Marketing Concept

Until the 1940s (discounting the depression years), American manufacturers could sell, with minimum effort, almost everything they could produce. There was more consumer demand for products than the manufacturers could supply. In the 1950s, after the recovery from World War II, the positions changed. Manufacturers, through improved facilities and technical breakthroughs, began to out-produce the consumer demand. It was an entirely new marketplace. Most consumers had the basic necessities of life. It was the discretionary dollar that now controlled the market. With increasing disposable income, the consumer could pick and choose among products and brands.

Manufacturers, to meet this new mood, developed and refined what is now called the "marketing concept." Simply put, the marketing concept is looking at the market from the consumer's point of view rather than the manufacturer's. This new marketing concept has had an important effect on the economy of our country because it shifted company emphasis from manufacturing and production to marketing. That, in turn, has had a dramatic effect on the importance of promotion, which resulted in the growth of advertising. Yet, even under these new conditions, we must keep advertising in the proper perspective. It's an important ingredient in the marketing mix, but it is usually only one ingredient among many as you will see in following examples.

The Difference Between
Marketing and Advertising

Marketing has been described by Jerome E. McCarthy as the management of the "Four Ps" — Product, Place, Price, and Promotion.[1] In other words, to develop a successful marketing plan there must be a Product available to the consumer at a Place for an acceptable Price with proper Promotion so the consumer knows of the product and its advantages. Thus, advertising is part of the company's promotion plan but usually not the only ingredient. Perhaps the following schematic of a marketing organization will put this thought in better perspective.

FIGURE 3-1

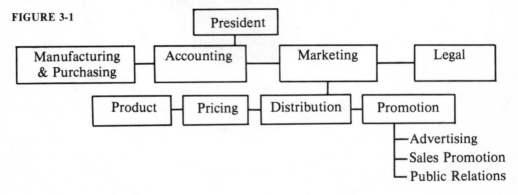

Taking the illustration a step further let's look at how the marketing director of an integrated marketing company probably looks at the marketing mix.[2] Again, note that advertising is just one of many factors which will affect the sale of the product. In addition, we must realize that for many types of products, particularly for those in the industrial area, advertising is usually only a minor factor in the final sale.

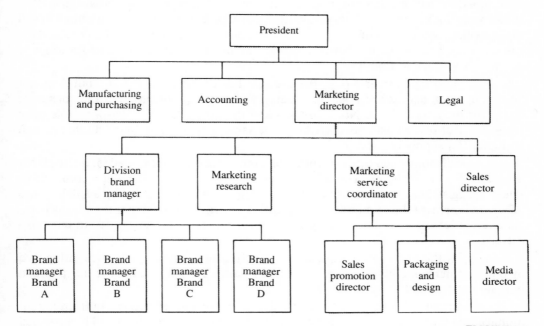

FIGURE 3-2

Evaluating Advertising in the Marketing Plan

It should now be clear that a total marketing program is necessary for the ultimate sale of a product or service. Advertising, while very important for certain products such as cosmetics, over-the-counter drugs and others, is only one of the tools used to make the marketing system function. Too often, it appears, we give advertising too much or too little credit for what it can accomplish in the overall sale of a product.

Almost everyone agrees the ultimate goal of advertising is to aid in the sale of a product. However, except under certain circumstances, such as direct mail or direct response advertising, it usually can't do the entire job. To understand advertising, we must keep the actual direct results in perspective.

While there is much discussion, many experts believe advertising should be evaluated on the basis of its communication ability and not just the sales record. There are simply too many intervening marketing variables between advertising and the ultimate sale to evaluate advertising results strictly on the basis of what happens at the cash register. Perhaps the following illustration will clarify the reasoning.

Let's assume we have just started an advertising campaign for a cold remedy. The campaign consists of a series of television commercials which direct the consumer to obtain the product at his favorite drug counter. Further assume that a person suffering from a cold saw our commercial and wanted the potential benefits which our product offered. As a direct result of the television commercial, the consumer decided to purchase our product on the way home from the office the following day.

The next day, the potential customer for our cold remedy stops at the first available drug store. The drug store owner, because he already stocks a number of other cold remedies, has decided not to stock our product. Thus, when our prospective consumer stops in for our brand, the druggist doesn't have it. He, instead, attempts to sell the consumer another brand. Because of our commercial, however, the consumer is still convinced he wants the benefits offered by our product and he decides to go to another drug store to find it.

At drug counter No. 2, the druggist has ordered our product but does not have it in stock because of a shipping delay. Still seeking our product, the consumer heads for drugstore No. 3. No. 3 had stocked the product, and it was available until yesterday. But seven customers arrived at the same time and purchased all that he had on hand. His supply is gone.

Still convinced by the commercial, our prospect is not disuaded; he heads for drugstore No. 4. While our commercials have promised our product at a competitive price, druggist No. 4, because he has so many other cold remedies available, has decided to increase the retail price to improve his margin. Thus, rather than being competitively priced, our product is 50 per cent higher than we had suggested in our commercial.

At the end of four trips, our cold-suffering consumer, who was influenced by our commercial, still hasn't been able to or hasn't chosen to purchase our product. No sale has resulted.

In spite of this, our advertising should be considered successful from a communications standpoint because the message we sent out was received and it persuaded the consumer to seek our brand. The advertising probably would have resulted in a sale had the product been available in the proper place at the proper time and at the proper price.

If we measured the communication effects of our commercial anywhere along the line, our advertising would have been judged effective. However, if we measured it strictly on the basis of a completed sale, it would have been unsuccessful. Thus, this simple situation illustrates the problems of trying to relate advertising directly to sales. In today's complex marketplace, it is even more difficult than this example shows.

From this illustration, the difference between marketing and advertising is quite clear. Marketing is all those factors which go into the sale of a product or service such as price, distribution, wholesale and retail support, plus advertising and promotion. Advertising is simply the communication of a sales or persuasive message designed to affect attitudes or behavior toward the advertised product. This difference becomes even more important as we begin to develop the creative message.

Understanding the Parts
of Advertising

Having differentiated between marketing and advertising, the next step is to differentiate the various steps of the advertising process. This is quite simple. Advertising consists of only two basic parts, the creative product or message and the medium or method used to get the message to the audience. While much more is involved in the development and placement of an advertisement, in a condensed form these two aspects make up the advertising process.

Recalling how advertising works, we know the primary goal of advertising is to get the right message to the right audience at the right time. The first part — the right message — has to do with the creative aspects of advertising. The second part — to the right audience at the right time — has to do with the function of the media. While both parts must work together for a successful advertising campaign, they are quite different. While one must help the other, neither can be successful without the other.

Initially, the message must be right. That is, it must offer a benefit or solve a consumer problem if it is to achieve its goal of changing mental attitudes or behavior. If the message is poorly designed, the best medium in the world won't make it successful.

Likewise, if an excellent message is developed but the medium directs the message to the wrong audience or no audience or it directs it at the wrong time, then success is doubtful. For example, assume we've developed an outstanding message about an acne product for teenagers. Through a misunderstanding, the medium selected to carry the message to the audience is a magazine about retirement activities. Obviously, few teenagers will read the retirement magazine. Thus, we could expect few results from our advertising message. The same problem could occur if we used an excellent advertising medium but developed a poor message.

To summarize, there are only two basic parts to advertising, the message or the creative product and the medium or message delivery. This important distinction is often forgotten, even by professionals. Remember, even if you have exclusive rights to the first guaranteed cure for cancer, if the advertising message is poorly developed or the medium is poorly chosen, sales success may not occur. A great medium can't compensate for a poor message and great creativity can have little effect unless the message is properly delivered.

Understanding Advertising
Objectives and Strategies

Having shown there are really only two parts to advertising, creative and media, the advertising business appears quite simple in concept. It's the doing that becomes complex, as we will see.

You'll recall we have stressed that advertising should be evaluated on the basis of communication effects, not sales results because there are many factors in the selling process over which advertising has no control. Therefore, it seems the only practical way to judge advertising is on the basis of its ability to deliver a sales message to an audience through the media. In other words, the desired effects of advertising should be attitudinal changes rather than behavioral.

The Lavidge and Steiner "Hierarchy of Effects" model has been recommended as a basis for advertising evaluation because it uses such attitudinal changes as awareness, knowledge, liking, preference, and conviction rather than just purchase. This model is important because it will help set advertising objectives and help relate them to advertising strategies.

Assume we develop an advertising campaign for underwater fly swatters, a totally new product. At this point, no one knows that our swatter exists. Thus, awareness, knowledge, liking, preference, conviction, and purchase are absent. If we telephoned 1,000 people, we wouldn't find anyone who knew about our product.

Therefore, we might set the following objectives for our underwater fly swatter advertising program to achieve within a period of six months:

1. Make 60 per cent of our target market aware our brand of underwater fly swatter exists.
2. Communicate knowledge of the purpose of our underwater fly swatter to 50 per cent of those in the target market who are aware the product exists.
3. Generate a liking for our product among 50 per cent of the 30 per cent who have heard about our underwater fly swatter.
4. Among the 15 per cent of the target market who are aware, know about, and like our underwater fly swatter, generate a 50 per cent preference for our product as an alternative to other ways of killing flies under water.
5. Among the 7.5 per cent who are aware, know about, like, and prefer our underwater fly swatter, have 50 per cent develop a *conviction* that they should buy it.

   At this point, the advertising objectives should logically stop because we have moved from the area of communication into the area of behavior. Usually, however, the full "Hierarchy of Effects" is completed. In this case, the final step might be:

6. Among the 3.75 per cent of the target market who are aware of, know about, like, prefer, and are convinced they should buy and use our underwater swatter, persuade 50 per cent to actually *purchase* it.

While the preceding example is extreme, it illustrates how logical advertising objectives can be set for a product. Obviously, if the product is already on the market, the advertising objectives would not start with a zero base. Usually, they are stated as an increase of awareness, knowledge, liking, etc. For example, for an aftershave lotion, the advertising objectives might be:

1. Increase awareness of the new wintergreen scent of Fred's aftershave lotion by 50 per cent among aftershave users.
2. Of those aftershave users who are aware of the new wintergreen scent, have 50 per cent know that only Fred's has that scent available.
3. . . . and, so on through the hierarchy.

Most advertisers cut down the number of steps they plan to measure to awareness, preference, and purchase intent. But, by now, you should clearly understand how advertising objectives are set.

Next we should concern ourselves with the key ingredient in setting advertising objectives — the message which is to be delivered. What do we want to say to customers and prospects? That's the creative strategy, the key ingredient in the advertising system. In Chapter 1, we defined an advertising strategy as:

> "The formulation of an advertising message that communicates the benefits or problem solution characteristics of the product or service to the market."

In other words, we're now dealing with "what we will say to the audience." It is this "what" that will make up the advertising objectives. For example, in the case of Fred's aftershave lotion, it's the new wintergreen scent that we want the audience to know about, not the price, the size of the package, the convenience, or anything else. Just the new scent. That's an important point. When developing an advertising strategy, it is usually best to have only one basic selling message. It is this single idea that forms our sales message and our creative strategy.

The difference between an advertising objective and an advertising strategy should be clear. The objective is the "effect" of the message or how much of "what we say" the audience sees or hears, remembers and reacts to. The advertising strategy is "what" we plan to say to them. These two concepts must be understood clearly because they form the underpinning of the balance of this text.

What's the Difference Between a Strategy and an Execution?

Having come this far, the end of the tunnel is now in sight. Admittedly the difference between strategies and executions is often confusing, even to a skilled advertising practitioner. It is, however, a skill that can be learned.

Referring to our definitions in Chapter 1 again, an advertising execution is:

> "The physical form in terms of art, illustration, copy, music, etc., in which the advertising strategy is presented to the target market to achieve the advertising objective(s)."

The advertising execution is "how" we plan to say something in contrast to "what" we say, which is the strategy. While this differentiation sounds simple, it isn't always quite so obvious. Perhaps an example will make the difference clearer. Let's say the creative or copy strategy for a cough remedy is to communicate to persons suffering from a sore throat that the advertised product offers a two-way benefit:

1. The cough remedy is antiseptic (kills germs).
2. The cough remedy is anesthetic (relieves pain).

This two-way benefit would be the general creative or advertising strategy for the product. In terms of execution, there may be literally hundreds of ways to communicate the message. For example, an animated television commercial might be used to show the remedy working in the throat; clinical tests might be presented; testimonials from satisfied customers might be used; a comparative demonstration of the product against competition might be a good idea and, the list could go on and on.

Further, these creative executions might take several media forms such as print, television, radio, or even point-of-purchase materials. The one unifying theme — in this case the two-way relief the cough remedy offers — is the creative strategy. How that message is communicated is an execution.

One major test can be used to determine if a creative idea is basically a strategy or an execution. Ask "how else could this message be presented using this idea?" If you are confusing executions with strategies, the answer will usually be "There's no other way. This is the only way it can be done." If this is the case, you're probably working with an execution, not a strategy. Remember, strategies can be executed in hundreds of ways, but there is only one way to describe an execution.

Chapter 4
Creative Strategies

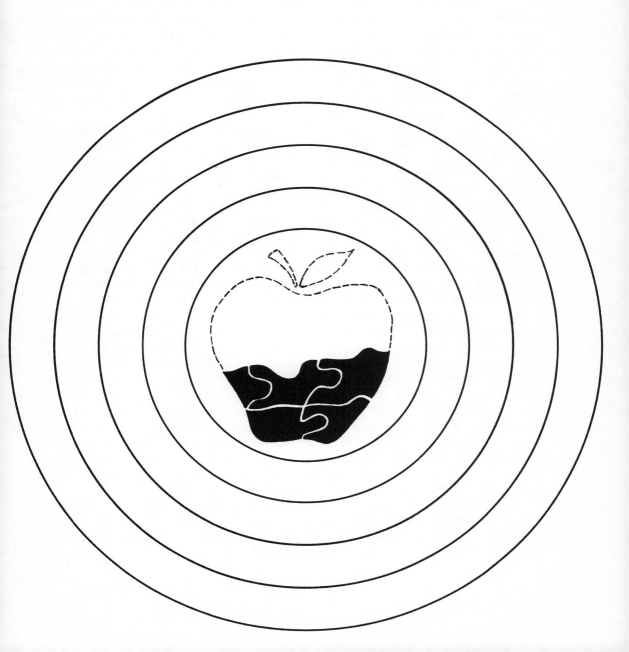

Essentials of Advertising Strategy

In the detergent section of almost any major supermarket, you can probably find most of the following brands on display, each with a different advertising strategy.

Brand	Advertising Strategy
Dreft	"The Detergent for Baby Laundry"
Ivory Snow	"Softens as it Cleans"
Gain	"A Clean You See, a Fresh You Smell"
Cheer	"The All-Temperature Detergent"
Bold	"Cleans Even Tough-to-Clean Modern Fabrics"
Tide	"Tide's In—Dirt's Out—America's Favorite"
Dash	"The Low Suds Concentrate"
Oxydol	"Bleaches as it Washes"

Why do we need all these different detergents? All are designed to do basically the same thing; they help remove dirt from clothing when used in an automatic washing machine. Why are there so many different brands? Why do they all have different claims? Why do they have different slogans? The reason is simple. Each brand was developed to fill a different market need. Some consumers want the advantages of a liquid detergent over a powder. Others prefer detergents with bleach. Still others want one that creates low suds. In other words, the detergent market is highly segmented in the mind of the consumer.

To serve these various markets, detergent manufacturers have developed a number of different product formulations. Each is designed to appeal to a different segment of the market. To communicate the benefits each brand offers, each has a different advertising or creative strategy. Each product is attempting to carve out a niche for itself among the many competitors in the market place. To gain a share, the brand must promise a different benefit or propose to solve a different problem of the consumer. But, there is one other thing all these detergent brands have in common. They're all manufactured by the same company, Procter & Gamble. P&G has almost perfected market positioning and advertising strategy development. All these brands compete in the detergent category and, to a certain extent, they compete among themselves. Primarily, however, they compete with other, non-P&G brands. To make this very fine distinction requires a very clear, very complete advertising strategy.

Many consumers obtain most of their knowledge about a product from advertising. Because there are at least 25 or more detergent brands on the market, the advertising strategy must clearly communicate the benefit the brand promises the consumer or the problem it is designed to solve. As you will note from the advertising strategies above, each brand has just such a claim or promise. The strategy clearly differentiates each brand.

P&G and its advertising agencies' skill in developing very distinct advertising strategies and then communicating them through advertisements is no accident. They are the experts in the field, the pioneers in market segmentation, product differentiation and advertising strategy. Their skill in this area is not limited only to detergents. It works in other areas too. P&G markets three separate dishwashing liquids, three all-purpose cleaners and at least six different brands of bar soap. All have carved out a place in the market. All have a loyal core of followers. But how did they do it? How did they develop advertising strategies that allow them to have eight different successful detergents in the market place? The answer is found in the strength and soundness of their creative advertising strategies.

The Importance of an Advertising Strategy

You may be asking just how important is an advertising strategy?

James R. Adams, co-founder of MacManus, John & Adams, Inc. (now D'Arcy MacManus & Masius), in his book *Sparks Off My Anvil,* described the importance of an advertising strategy this way:

> "If I had to lay down one rule for improving American advertising, I would specify that advertising men take more time to work out their underlying purposes and objectives. Being primarily creative, they are too anxious to draw pictures and write copy. They are inclined to fire before they see the whites of their public's eyes! The great advantage which some advertisers enjoy over others lies largely in superior strategy. Most American advertising is good in its purely creative aspects. Visualization is of a uniformly high average, and copy is written with a fair degree of craftsmanship. But the difference in the effectiveness of the strategy employed is the difference between day and night. In fact, much advertising has no strategy whatever. This is due to lack of appreciation on the part of many as to what strategy can accomplish. What you are trying to do is far more important than how you do it."[1]

That is why we start the advertising process with strategy. It's much more exciting to start writing ads than strategies largely because strategies require thinking. Judging by some of the television commercials and radio spots which have appeared lately, writing commercials must require absolutely no thinking.

It's All in the Advertising Strategy

Let's refer once again to our basic definition of an advertising strategy:

> "The formulation of an advertising message that communicates the benefit or problem-solution characteristics of the product or service to the market."

The key words here are "benefit or problem solution characteristics." If the promise of the advertising strategy doesn't fill a consumer need, solve a consumer problem, or offer a desired consumer benefit, it will fail. Also note that the promise made in the strategy must be important to the consumer, not to the manufacturer or advertiser. For example, some consumers obviously believe they need and want a "low sudsing detergent" such as Dash. Others want the bleaching action of Oxydol, while still others believe that softness in the wash, such as Ivory Snow promises, is the most important feature in a detergent.

You'll recall we said in Chapter 2 that advertising consists of three steps: (1) getting the right message (2) to the right audience (3) at the right time. The advertising strategy has to do with the first step, developing "the right message." But how do you develop the right message? How do you know it's right? How do you know consumers will respond to the message? In short, what makes a good advertising strategy and how do you go about developing one?

What Makes a Good Advertising Strategy?

There are four basic ingredients for a sound advertising strategy.

1. The strategy must offer a *consumer* benefit or solve a *consumer* problem.
2. The benefit offered or the solution promised must be wanted or desired by the consumer.

3. The brand must be tied directly to the benefit or the problem solution offered.
4. The benefit or problem solution must be communicable through media advertising.

We'll look at each of these ingredients separately.

The Strategy Must Offer a Consumer Benefit or Solve a Consumer Problem

All advertising promises something, i.e. "Purchase this product or service and you will get this benefit." It's as simple as that. Unfortunately, many messages masquerade as advertising and fail because they can't or don't make this simple promise. Glance through any magazine or newspaper. You'll find a multitude of advertisements which either don't make a promise or garble the message so badly the consumer can't see the benefit or problem solution hidden amidst the clever words and beautiful pictures. The advertising strategy must be clear, complete, and offer a benefit or solve a consumer problem. If it doesn't, then it isn't a sound advertising strategy.

Let's look at P&G's detergents more closely. Through research, P&G has discovered the detergent market is highly segmented. In other words, consumers seek different benefits or solutions to washday problems through their detergents. Not all are the same. To take advantage of these diverse consumer needs and wants, P&G developed different product formulations. Creative strategies were developed to communicate the advantages of the different brands.

FIGURE 4-1. Gain promises "A clean you see, a fresh you can smell" in its advertising.

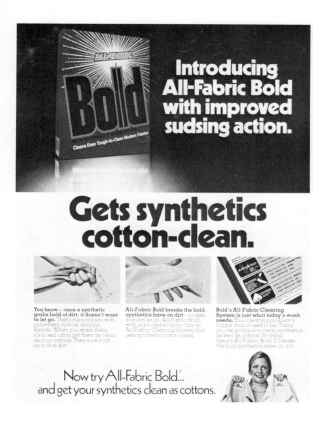

Introducing All-Fabric Bold with improved sudsing action.

Gets synthetics cotton-clean.

You know — once a synthetic grabs hold of dirt, it doesn't want to let go. That's the problem with polyesters, nylons, acrylics, blends. When you wash them, it's a real job to get them as clean as your cottons. They sure hold on to that dirt.

All-Fabric Bold breaks the hold synthetics have on dirt — makes that dirt let go. All-Fabric Bold, with improved sudsing, has an All-Fabric Cleaning System that gets synthetics cotton-clean.

Bold's All-Fabric Cleaning System is just what today's wash needs. Your cleaning problem's bigger than it used to be. Today you've got hard-to-clean synthetics as well as cottons. So today there's All-Fabric Bold. It breaks the hold synthetics have on dirt.

Now try All-Fabric Bold... and get your synthetics clean as cottons.

FIGURE 4-2. Bold's creative strategy is built around its "Cleans even tough-to-clean modern fabrics" slogan.

For example, Gain promises clean clothes and a fresh smell. P&G, through research has apparently found that some consumers judge the cleanliness of their wash on the basis of smell. Therefore, Gain promises "fresh smell" when clothes are laundered with that product. It is also apparent a large number of consumers have difficulty getting new synthetic fabrics clean in their laundry. So Bold makes the claim "Cleans even tough-to-clean modern fabrics." Cheer, recognizing most families have a variety of clothing, made of different fabrics, requiring different water temperatures, offers the benefit of a single "All-temperature" detergent for all types of laundry.

While each product has a different formulation and a different creative strategy that communicates the specific benefit, the final judgment will be based on consumer use. In other words, the consumer must feel the product delivers the benefit which the creative strategy promises.

Thus, we see that creative strategies must be firmly rooted in (a) finding a market segment which seeks the product benefits, (b) communicating that benefit through a clear, concise creative strategy, and (c) delivering the promised benefit so the consumer will continue to purchase the product.

The Benefit Offered or the Solution Promised
Must Be Wanted or Desired by Consumers

Too often, it seems, manufacturers or advertisers develop product benefits which they feel are important but about which the consumer cares little. Advertising history, however, has shown it is imperative the consumer desire the benefit.

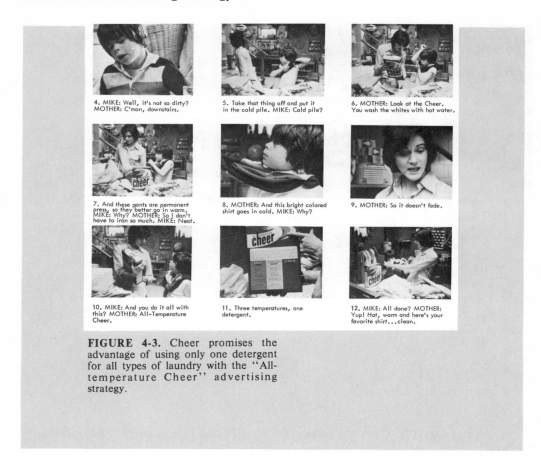

4. MIKE: Well, it's not so dirty? MOTHER: C'mon, downstairs.

5. Take that thing off and put it in the cold pile. MIKE: Cold pile?

6. MOTHER: Look at the Cheer. You wash the whites with hot water.

7. And these pants are permanent press, so they better go in warm. MIKE: Why? MOTHER: So I don't have to iron so much. MIKE: Neat.

8. MOTHER: And this bright colored shirt goes in cold. MIKE: Why?

9. MOTHER: So it doesn't fade.

10. MIKE: And you do it all with this? MOTHER: All-Temperature Cheer.

11. Three temperatures, one detergent.

12. MIKE: All done? MOTHER: Yup! Hot, warm and here's your favorite shirt...clean.

FIGURE 4-3. Cheer promises the advantage of using only one detergent for all types of laundry with the "All-temperature Cheer" advertising strategy.

To show you what we mean, assume you manufacture wooden clothespins. Sales have been declining, and you must find a way to rescue the business. You put your research and development people to work on the problem. Your laboratory experts find a way to dye your wooden clothespins various colors. What a breakthrough this is. People can have color-coordinated clothespins for a colorful washline.

You could even offer the benefit that people could match various colors in their laundry with the clothespins and be the envy of the neighborhood. Even more important, you can patent the dying process so none of your competitors can copy your colored clothespins. You think you've rescued the business. The only thing you need to do is advertise the colored clothespins and consumers are sure to flock to your brand. After all, no one else can match your dying process. You have an exclusive benefit.

Is this a good advertising strategy? Probably not. You've looked at the benefit only from your side. Sure, only you can manufacture the colored clothespins. Colored clothespins probably would be attractive on the line. But the question is, does the consumer care? Would colored clothespins be a benefit to the woman who is washing and hanging four loads of laundry a week? Is she concerned about the attractiveness of her clothespins or is she more concerned about finding a clothespin that will hold her husband's heavy work clothes in a strong wind? In this case, the benefit is all from the manufacturer's side, not the consumer's.

The benefit of colored clothespins is probably not important. The fact that only you offer the benefit doesn't make it any more important to the consumer. Here then, is an example of a company benefit, not a consumer benefit. A stronger clothespin might be the solution to a problem. A colored clothespin probably isn't.

The main point here is that the benefit must be of value to the consumer or solve a consumer problem, otherwise it will not lead to an effective advertising strategy.

Jim Adams, in his book *Sparks Off My Anvil,* had this to say about manufacturer versus consumer benefits:

> "You must know what it is you are trying to get people to believe about your product or your organization before you can accomplish much. But often, even when this fact is known and remembered, a mistake is made in setting up the advertising goal. The advertiser often tries to get people to believe the wrong thing — or a thing which is not the most effective one that could be advertised. When this mistake occurs, it is generally because the people who are doing the advertising thinking are thinking backwards. They start out by thinking first about themselves and their product, instead of thinking about the people they are trying to induce to buy the product. Sales are made in the heads of people. Consequently, in arriving at a proper advertising strategy, you have to start with the emotions of your prospects and work back to your product. You have to figure out what people would have to believe about your product in order to give it outstanding preference over all others of its kind. Otherwise, you may succeed in getting your advertising believed — and still accomplish nothing!
>
> No product ever manufactured was of the slightest interest to anybody, purely within itself — except, perhaps to its maker.
>
> A product becomes interesting and desirable only when translated into terms of human satisfaction."[2]

This was written more than 20 years ago, but it is just as true now as it ever has been. If you want to develop sound advertising strategies and write effective advertising, *START WHERE YOUR CUSTOMER IS, NOT WHERE YOU ARE.*

The Benefit or Problem Solution Must Be Tied to the Brand

The benefit or problem solution must be so closely associated with the brand's advertising that no competitor can effectively make the same claim. It doesn't do much good to develop a benefit or problem solution which is generic to the entire category. For example, another P&G brand, Coast, is a deodorant bar soap with a heavy aroma. The advertising strategy is "a refreshing bathing experience." The strategy is executed with the line "Coast brings you back to life." Thus, the benefit is a refreshing, wake-up bath with Coast.

Through advertising, Coast has established itself as the "refreshing bath soap." Because Coast is using this advertising strategy, no other bar soap could or would want to make that claim or offer that benefit. Coast has linked its advertising strategy directly to the brand in a clear and concise way.

Another example of strongly linking an advertising strategy to a brand is

Ivory bar soap, another P&G brand. For over 100 years, P&G has used the same advertising strategy for Ivory. It is known as being a pure, mild soap because of its slogan "99 and 44/100 per cent pure. It floats." The advertising strategy has become so firmly linked to Ivory that no other brand could ever infringe on the pureness, mildness strategy. The benefit and the brand are inexorably intertwined.

The Benefit or Problem Solution Must Be Communicable Through Media Advertising

A sound advertising strategy must be communicable through media advertising. That sounds almost trite, but unfortunately some advertising strategies are developed that cannot or are difficult to communicate in a media form. The limitations of the media must be recognized.

Some things simply can't be done or can't be communicated effectively through media channels. Personal demonstrations often fall into this category, particularly those which require a period of time. Other things must be experienced physically, such as smell. While most advertising strategies can be executed in one way or another in the media, guard against those which can't. A strategy which can't be communicated is worse than no strategy at all.

Chapter 5
How To Develop An Advertising Strategy

With this understanding of advertising strategy, how do you go about developing one? Is there a formula? Are there a series of steps which can be taken? Are some strategies better than others?

While we say yes, the answer isn't all that clear-cut. Advertising practitioners have suggested several approaches to developing advertising strategies. As you might expect, the person who had success with one form of strategy believes it to be the best. Other experts disagree. Let's look at several alternatives which have proven successful over the years.

Most articles about advertising strategy use illustrations of campaigns or executions to support specific positions on strategy development. For example, the writer may outline how a specific advertising campaign was developed or how individual advertisements were conceived. In most instances, the acceptance of a particular method of developing a creative advertising strategy is primarily a result of the success of the careers of its advocates and/or the products for which the campaigns were developed.

It seems each new, successful advertising campaign has brought forth a "new school of advertising." Because of its success, the campaign is often widely imitated by others seeking the same success. Unfortunately, because most advertising campaigns are product, time, and situation specific, the examples cited have no relevant parallel in current practice. Further, these campaigns or executions are used to explain a strategy rather than to show how the strategy resulted in the execution. This approach is almost backward.

There have been, however, some very successful conceptualizers in the field of advertising strategy. One must usually go beyond the specific examples to find the basis for the creative strategy approach. For example, in the 1940s, Rosser Reeves suggested the use of the "Unique Selling Proposition," which was credited with the growth of Ted Bates & Co. In the 1950s and 1960s, David Ogilvy of Ogilvy & Mather Inc. had much success with "Brand Image." In the 1970s, the creative strategy approach was "Positioning," advocated by Jack Trout and Al Ries of Ries, Cappiello, Colwell. There have been others, but these three approaches are the most widely accepted. Each is explained below.

The Unique Selling Proposition

In his book *Reality in Advertising,* Rosser Reeves, then at Ted Bates & Co., outlined the now famous "Unique Selling Proposition" or USP which is widely used as a basis for advertising strategy development. Reeves described the USP as having three parts:

1. Each advertisement must make a proposition to the consumer. Not just words, not just product puffery, not just show-window advertising. Each advertisement must say to each reader: 'Buy this product and you will get this specific benefit' . . .
2. The proposition must be one that the competition either cannot, or does not, offer. It must be unique either in the brand or the claim . . .
3. The proposition must be strong enough to move the mass million, i.e., pull over new customers to your product . . . [1]

What would be a strategy using a USP? Reeves used the example of Colgate toothpaste, which at that time was claiming "Cleans your breath as it cleans your teeth." This was the first time a toothpaste had claimed both teeth cleaning and breath freshening. Other products with a USP that immediately come to mind are the Polaroid camera, which promises instant color photographs; DuPont's Teflon coating, which promises no-stick cooking convenience; Kava coffee, which has been acid-neutralized; Chicken of the Sea tuna, which has been federally inspected; Wisk liquid laundry detergent, which stops "Ring around the collar," and, finally, Mobil 1, the synthetic motor oil that promises improved gas mileage.

The Brand Image

A second approach to advertising strategy development was best demonstrated by David Ogilvy in his book *Confessions of an Advertising Man*. Ogilvy recommended "Brand Image" as a method of developing sound advertising strategies. He stated that every advertisement is a long-term investment in the overall makeup of the brand.[2]

FIGURE 5-1. Polaroid continues its development of new technical breakthroughs which result in a built-in "Unique Selling Proposition" for their products. A recent example is the "ONESTEP" camera. In this case, the "Unique Selling Proposition" is one which competitors can't or are unable to duplicate rapidly thus giving Polaroid a definite selling edge. This comes through clearly in the advertising approach.

How come only one leading tuna has this Gov't. seal of approval?

Chicken of the Sea® is the only leading tuna that voluntarily requests constant federal inspection.

There's no law that requires us to have a federal inspector constantly on the job.

But we do it for a good reason. We think it's the best way to reassure you and your family that our delicious tuna is consistently wholesome, top-quality tuna. Can after can.

Chicken of the Sea. It's the only leading tuna with a Government seal of approval because it's the only one that earns it.

Chicken of the Sea.

© Ralston Purina Company, 1978

FIGURE 5-2. Chicken of the Sea tuna has developed a USP by taking advantage of voluntary federal inspection. The proposition is "unique" because Chicken of the Sea is the only leading brand of tuna which has this inspection. It's a "selling proposition" because it offers the consumer a benefit, a guarantee of consistently good tuna. That's a USP the consumer can see, understand, and believe.

The general idea is that an image can be developed for every product. Based on this image, the consumer doesn't buy the product; he buys the physical and psychological benefits the product promises to deliver. As a result, what is said about the product is more important than its physical attributes. Because the benefits of an advertising strategy based on "Brand Image" are often psychological, they are sometimes subject to rapid change as society evolves. Brand imagery, however, does offer strong opportunities for strategy development for many types of products.

Many examples of brand imagery have been developed by Ogilvy and his agency. For instance: The man in the Hathaway shirt with the eye-patch, the pride of a Rolls-Royce automobile, Commander Whitehead representing Sweppes mixes, the thundering herd of bulls for Merrill Lynch and the old-fashioned style of Pepperidge Farms bakery goods.

Get up to 10 extra miles out of a tankful of gas.

Now there's an *oil* that saves you gas.

It's called Mobil 1 and it reduces engine friction so well, it will take the average car up to 10 extra miles per tankful. But the miracle of Mobil 1 doesn't stop there.

Being synthetic, Mobil 1 protects your engine better than ordinary motor oil.

To prove it, we put Mobil 1 in a fleet of highway patrol cars for 12,000 miles, adding oil as needed. We then tested the "used" Mobil 1 against brand-new motor oils and found that even used, Mobil 1 protected like the ordinary new oils.

Mobil 1 also improves cold weather starts and also works well in high temperatures.

At 35 degrees below zero, it will continue to flow and help you start easier.

And Mobil 1 doesn't thin out in a running engine the way ordinary oils do, even in the scorching heat of summer.

Finally, the oil that saves you gas also saves you oil. In both city and highway fleet tests, Mobil 1 cut oil consumption up to 25%.

You can't buy a better motor oil than this one.

Mobil 1 The oil that saves you gas.

FIGURE 5-3. Mobil 1 motor oil offers a "Unique Selling Proposition" by promising to give extra gas mileage. Being the first manufacturer to use this claim, Mobil has pre-empted competitive products that follow.

Essentials of Advertising Strategy

Leo Burnett Co., U.S.A., advertising agency has used brand imagery effectively, too, for priority products. It has used trade characters to identify certain products, such as the Marlboro man, Tony the Tiger for Kellogg's Frosted Flakes and the Jolly Green Giant for vegetables. All these are solid examples of the power of a creative strategy built on "Brand Image."

Although it sometimes is not readily apparent when brand imagery is used to develop a creative strategy, the image still must offer a consumer benefit or solve a consumer problem. The use of a character or an image must be directly related in some way to this even if it is only a psychological benefit.

Referring back to our examples of image strategy, the benefit of the Hathaway shirt was that it was worn by distinguished men. Thus, if the consumer purchased and wore a Hathaway shirt, the psychological benefit would be the distinction of wearing the shirt. The same is true for Marlboro. The image of the cigarette was distinctive, and the psychological advantages were many — masculinity, outdoor freshness, the "Old West" look, etc. Remember, though, the "Brand Image" must offer a benefit or solve a consumer problem to be effective.

6. Merrill Lynch.

7. All around

8. America...

10. turn to Merrill Lynch than any other investment firm.

11. (SFX: BULLS STAMPEDE) Sure, there are lots of investment firms.

12. But there's only one Merrill Lynch. (MUSIC OUT)

FIGURE 5-4. The Merrill Lynch "Bulls" have brilliantly translated the creative strategy of this brokerage firm during the past few years. Being "Bullish on America" has been a most successful approach.

MAN: (OC) Whoa!!!!

Timmy! I got some delivery today:

Bread like it used to be -

baked fresh with no artificial
preservatives.

molasses, honey,

'n no artificial preservatives.

FIGURE 5-5. The old-fashioned,
homey appeal of Pepperidge Farm products comes through in the "Brand
Image" presentation of the country
baker and his wagon.

With rapid technological advancement and the ability of competition to duplicate products, "Unique Selling Proposition's" are becoming more and more difficult to develop. Many advertisers, therefore, are leaning more toward the development of an image for their brand as an advertising strategy. A strong "brand image" approach can provide a sound creative strategy for many products.

Positioning as an Advertising Strategy

In 1972, Jack Trout and Al Ries, then of Ries, Cappiello, Colwell, a New York advertising agency, wrote a series of articles which ran in *Industrial Marketing* and later in *Advertising Age,* describing a new approach to advertising strategy development called "Positioning." "Positioning" is different from the USP or "Brand Image" approach. Because of the success of "Positioning" the Trout and Ries approach has been widely accepted and used.

Originally, according to Trout and Ries, "Positioning" was what the manufacturer did to his product to create benefits for a specific group of people. "Positioning" now, however, has taken on a different meaning. As Trout and Ries described it, "Positioning" is what the advertising does for the product in the prospect's mind.

FIGURE 5-6. The "Marlboro Man" successfully changed the image of what was previously a "feminine appearing" cigarette. Originally the identifying symbol was built around a "tattoo," but the western motif has slowly evolved through the years. The approach and actors may change, but the "Brand Image" is maintained.

The general concept is that advertising is used to gain a foothold or occupy a place for a product in the mind of the consumer. Once that position is established, the consumer should consider the product any time he needs the type of benefit or problem solution the product offers. Rather than advertising a product that has specific advantages, "Positioning" works to make the product fill all the needs of the consumer in a particular category or area.[3]

One example of sound "Positioning" cited by Trout and Ries is the "We're No. 2" position of Avis Rent-A-Car. By taking that position, Avis was able to claim it kept its cars cleaner, in better mechanical condition and it gave better service than the market leader, Hertz. Because it was trying to catch up, Avis was advertised as working harder.

Another product position that worked very well was 7 Up's "Un-Cola" strategy. It allowed 7 Up, which had a confusing position in the market, to establish itself as the alternative soft drink to the major colas, Coca-Cola and Pepsi-Cola.

Michelob beer took the "first class" position to establish itself as the first American-made premium beer. Schaefer beer established itself as the brand for the heavy beer drinker by positioning itself as "The one beer to have when you're having more than one." And, to return once again to Procter & Gamble, it took the leading position in toothpaste by obtaining the American Dental Association's Seal of Approval for Crest. With this authoritative position, Crest has never lost its market-leading spot.

Just as with brand imagery or a USP, "Positioning" must offer the consumer a benefit or solve a consumer problem. Unless the "Positioning" does this, the advertising will not be successful.

Strategies That Almost Never Work

Having reviewed some of the methods of developing advertising strategies, some things must be said about an area of advertising for which almost no strategy can be developed. It's often called "corporate advertising," which is used by organizations to express a point of view, clarify a position, or explain a situation to the "public." A prime example of this approach was the advertising used by oil companies during the energy crisis of the mid-1970s. In an attempt to explain the "windfall profits" which occurred during that period, oil companies ran ads and commercials attempting to justify their positions. Generally, the effort failed because of poor advertising strategies. The oil companies attempted to defend a position which offered no benefit to the consumer and certainly didn't solve a consumer problem. In some instances, the oil companies advertising may have even intensified the problems.

The primary consumer problems at the time these advertisements appeared were a shortage of gasoline, fuel oil and natural gas *plus* skyrocketing prices. The oil companies explanation of how the "windfall profits" occured did nothing to solve those problems. It didn't create more gasoline. It didn't generate more fuel oil. It didn't provide more natural gas. And, it certainly didn't do anything about lowering the price of the products. Thus, we see an example of an advertising strategy which probably backfired because it wasn't built on a consumer benefit or didn't solve a consumer problem.

Many attempts at corporate advertising face the same problems. Companies try to tell consumers something they have little interest in or which does not deal

2. MAMA: Tony! TONY: Mama!

3. MAMA: You look hungry.
Come start your good breakfast,

5. The secret frosting makes
it extra crunchy,...

6. ...extra delicious.

8. MAMA: How did I teach
you to say it?

9. TONY: It's grrrrrrrreat!

11. ...to the rest of the world,
but you know what you are to me.

12. TONY: Your little Tony?

FIGURE 5-7. "Tony the Tiger" has
been building and maintaining the
"Brand Image" for Kellogg's Frosted
Flakes for nearly a quarter of a century.
It's done "Grrrreatt!" things for the
brand.

specifically with a direct consumer benefit. When this occurs, the company is often talking to itself. This is not to say corporations cannot communicate with consumers through advertising. They can. But to do so, the message they use must be based on an advertising strategy that offers a consumer benefit or solves a consumer problem.

When developing an advertising strategy, you must always keep the consumer at the forefront. The acid test of any strategy is "What benefit or what solution to what problem will this provide for the consumer?" If the answer is "none" or "little," start looking for another strategy. The one you have usually won't work.

FIGURE 5-8. Probably one of the best known of all trade characters is the "Jolly Green Giant" for Green Giant Foods. The "Brand Image" has enabled Green Giant to successfully differentiate its vegetable products over the years.

51

(MUSIC THROUGHOUT)
SONG: (UNdo it with 7UP) It's the same thing, only different

(UNdo it)

It's a fresher kind of style

(UNdo it with 7UP)

A more natural way

of doin' things

(UNdo it)

A more natural way

of doin' things

GIRL'S VOICE: I'd call it the feature attraction.

SONG: Yeah, the only way to do it is

UNdo it. 7UP!
SUPER: UNdo it (7UP).

FIGURE 5-9. 7UP had a confusing image among many consumers. Some thought it was a "mixer," others a fruit drink, but few thought of it as an alternative soft drink. The "Un-Cola" positioning successfully described exactly what the product was in the marketplace.

FIGURE 5-10. Michelob successfully positioned itself as the first American-made premium beer. "First-class in beer" now means Michelob. While other brands, including imports, have attempted to take the Michelob position, none has been successful.

The jeans with the fancy stitching on the back pocket are the world's best-selling jeans. They cost about $15.00. The jeans on the right are JCPenney Plain Pockets. They cost $10.00. Which would you rather have? A half-cent's worth of stitching on your pocket, or $5.00 in your pocket.

Plain Pocket Jeans only at **JCPenney**

Also through the catalog.

FIGURE 5-11. J.C. Penney is attempting to take the lower price but same quality" position against the market leader with this advertising for "Plain Pockets Jeans." The consumer benefit is clear in the lines "Which would you rather have? A half-cent's worth of stitching on the pocket, or $5.00 *in* your pocket."

FIGURE 5-12. Advertising for Revlon's "Charlie" has positioned it as the fragrance and cosmetics line for a specific kind of woman. The "Charlie" girl is always found in the midst of "excitement."

FIGURE 5-13. Yuban has been successfully positioned as "one of the richest coffees you can buy," supported through all elements of the advertising campaign.

Chapter 6
Steps In Strategy Development

It's almost time to take pencil in hand and start writing an advertising strategy. We've covered the basic approaches to strategy development: USP, brand imagery, and positioning. The importance of having the strategy offer a benefit or solve a problem for the consumer, not the company, has been stressed.

But to develop an effective strategy a few more elements are necessary. First, you must understand the idea of where customers come from or the idea of a target market. Second, it's vital to know how to obtain market information for use in strategy development. Let's look at each point briefly.

Where Do Customers Come From?

The question sounds simple enough. But where *do* customers come from? Aren't they just out there? Don't they just exist in the marketplace, with your only job being to let them know your strategy? Well, not quite.

For any type of product or service, all customers or prospects can be found in one of the three market segments illustrated below:[1]

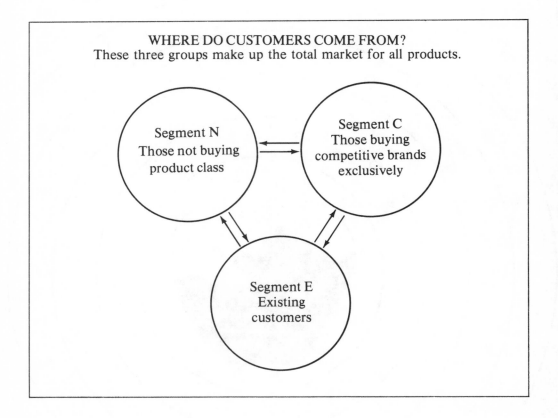

WHERE DO CUSTOMERS COME FROM?
These three groups make up the total market for all products.

Segment N
Those not buying
product class

Segment C
Those buying
competitive brands
exclusively

Segment E
Existing
customers

Group N is those consumers who are not buying anything in your product category. In other words, if you were in the automatic washer detergent business, these would be people who didn't own a washer, did not use a detergent, or perhaps never washed their clothes. For whatever reason, they aren't using any brand of washer detergent.

Group C, on the other hand, comprises those consumers who buy competitive brands exclusively. They use automatic washer detergents, but they always buy a brand other than. yours. Usually, they've never even tried your brand.

Group P is the present customers for your brand. These people buy your detergent either exclusively or on a regular basis so that you can count them as customers.

As the illustration shows, these three segments make up the entire market. Note, however, as indicated by the arrows, the market is not stagnant. People move from one group to another. These moves are based on their needs or, hopefully, on your advertising strategy and execution.

How do people move in this sort of a marketplace? First, people in Group N can start using automatic washer detergents. They may buy an automatic washer, start using a laundromat, or just start washing their clothes. When they do change, they have two choices. They can go to a competitive brand (Group C) or they can become your customer (Group P).

The same thing can happen with your present customers, Group P. If your product fails to satisfy the consumer's needs, one of two things will happen. They will either entirely stop using automatic washer detergents or they will start using a competitive brand. And similar movement occurs in Group C. They may move out of the market or start using your brand.

By seeing this make-up of the marketplace, you should gain a clearer understanding of the importance of the advertising strategy. In order to develop a specific advertising strategy, you need to identify to whom the strategy is directed.

More than likely, a claim that your brand of detergent will get clothes cleaner and brighter would be of little direct interest to those people in Group N. They don't use detergents. Why would a claim of cleaner, brighter washes from your detergent appeal to them?

On the other hand, the cleaner, brighter wash might be of interest to those people in Group C. They use other brands of detergents. If they are unhappy with their present brand or don't feel their clothes are clean and bright enough, they might find this a desirable benefit or it might solve a washday problem.

The message of cleaner, brighter clothes from using your detergent has two logical audiences, people in Group C who are using another brand and your own customers who might need to be reminded that your detergent gives them a clean, bright wash.

If you were to develop an advertising strategy for Group N, you'd have to identify why the people are not using detergents. If it is because they don't own a washing machine, your chances of converting them are slim indeed. If, however, the problem is that they believe detergents destroy the fabric in their clothes, you might develop an advertising strategy which speaks to that point, i.e., your brand of detergent is gentle to clothing and it doesn't destroy the fabric. The advertising strategy, in addition to offering a specific consumer benefit or solving a consumer problem, must be directed to the segment of the market to whom that strategy might appeal.

Where Do You Get Market Information?

Usually information for the development of a sound, effective strategy comes from advertising research information. While all aspects of marketing and advertising research are too detailed to discuss here, some of the many research services that provide market information should be mentioned. These services, many of them syndicated, provide many details on the various segments of the market, including such information as who uses what products, how much they use, when they use it, what size they purchase, how the product is used, etc. These are vital factors in the development of an effective creative strategy.

There are many sources of market and consumer information. Two of the primary sources of basic consumer usage information are W. R. Simmons & Co. and Simmons Market Research Bureau and the M.R.C.A. Menu Census for various consumer products. Both services are available by subscription only. Often, however, they publish information about general market categories.

The U.S. Census also provides a wealth of free information on all types of market information. Often, trade publications such as *Progressive Grocer, Supermarket News, Advertising Age,* and others publish special articles on usage and consumption of various products. The best source of information is often a good market research text or the local library.

One source of information often overlooked, especially by beginners, is personal information. Nothing takes the place of actually visiting retail outlets where the product is sold. Talk to consumers. Ask them why they buy or don't buy specific brands. Ask them what they would like to see in a product. What they would like to see changed. What's important to them in making a purchase decision.

Two Common Mistakes in Advertising Strategy Development

One of the most common mistakes in advertising strategy development is attempting to talk to too large a market or to too many people. Many times, when you attempt to talk to a very large group, you end up talking to no one in particular. Advertising is one-to-one communication. The media are only the vehicles for this personal presentation.

Sometimes you will fall into the trap of thinking that because your advertisement will be read by or your commercial will be seen by millions of people, you must say something of interest to all of them. Not so. Each person who sees or hears your advertising reacts to it individually and usually differently. This can't be stressed enough. Advertising uses the mass media but only for one-to-one communication. Don't confuse mass audiences with mass messages.

Along the same line, the second common mistake in developing an advertising strategy is trying to cram too many ideas into it, too many selling points. For the most part, an advertising strategy should contain only one selling message. Your strategy should have one primary benefit or solve one major problem. When you start hanging additional benefits on the strategy to include other segments of the market, you weaken the entire strategy.

If you believe it is important to speak to another group of consumers about a different benefit or to offer another problem solution with your product, write another strategy directed to that audience. Don't try to expand your benefit to fit the entire market. It just won't work.

Six Steps to Developing an Advertising Strategy

With these two common mistakes firmly in mind, here's a step by step method of developing an advertising strategy.

THE ADVERTISING STRATEGY OUTLINE

1. Define Your Product or Service
2. Define Your Target Market
   A. Geographics
   B. Demographics
   C. Psychographics
   D. Media Patterns
   E. Buying/Use Patterns
3. USP/Positioning/Identity
4. Additional Selling Points
5. Technique
6. Define Your Advertising Objectives

This guide (worksheets are included at the end of the book) has been used by advertisers and advertising agencies across the country. Why? Because it works. And, it can work for you.

Before explaining how to use the outline, a suggestion based on experience is necessary. It works best if you write the strategy with one person in mind. That is, pick out a person who would be a representative prospect for your product. Develop your strategy as if you were going to write specifically to that one person. It will help you get a better idea of what you want to do, the actual benefit you want to offer to the person or the problem which the product is to solve. It also helps you best structure your strategy to communicate your message.

This "one person" strategy is primarily a teaching technique for the beginner. As you gain experience, you'll learn to group people for convenience because media usually can't be purchased to reach only one person. However, the technique does help you keep in mind that your advertising strategy and ultimately your execution are being seen, read or heard by only one person at a time. Think in terms of one person. You'll find it much easier than talking to a crowd.

Now, here's how to use the advertising strategy outline to develop a sound creative strategy.

Step One: The first step is to understand thoroughly the product or service you plan to advertise. While this sounds elementary, you'd be surprised how many advertising planners start developing a strategy without fully understanding the product or service with which they are working.

A cardinal rule is to use the product yourself whenever possible. Try not to depend on an explanation from other people to tell you how the product works or what it does. If at all possible, use the product for several days. See how it works. What are its strong points? Its weaknesses? Does it do what you say it will do? Every time? Put it to the ultimate consumer test yourself because your customers will.

Next, think about what your product will do for the consumer. What benefit does it offer? What problem does it solve? Put this in consumer language, not technical jargon. If someone asked you to explain what your product or service did, could you do it in two sentences? What would you say? You must be that simple and that direct.

Essentials of Advertising Strategy

Often the product isn't just a bundle of physical benefits. Sometimes it's emotional or psychological. Once when Charles Revson, founder of Revlon, Inc., the cosmetics company, was asked to describe what he sold, he said simply, "We sell women hope." In other words, Revson saw his company not as a producer or distributor of nail polish, perfume, lipstick, or other cosmetics, but as a company that promised women a better life through the use of its products.

Look at your product or service the same way. Look beyond the mere physical benefits. What are the intangible benefits of your products or services? What problems can they solve to give the user a better life? Describe your product or service in those terms.

Step Two: Now it is time to define your target market. Who is the primary person to whom your message will be directed? The better you can describe that person, the better you will understand how to develop an advertising strategy that will appeal to that person. The strategy outline requires you to describe your target market in several ways. Again, remember it's best if you can direct your strategy to one person. Therefore, try to imagine the specific person who is a logical prospect for your product. Describe that person.

First describe where the target person lives geographically. It makes a great deal of difference whether your target lives in Florida or in Maine. The weather is different, the housing is different, the jobs are different, and the people are different. If possible, describe the type of town or city where your prime prospect resides. People living in Atlanta often are much different than people living in Dime Box, Texas.

A prime example of the important way geography can affect an advertising strategy is thermal underwear. People in Duluth, Minn. know and understand thermal underwear. They know the product and how it should and must be used in their climate. People in San Diego, however, have little use for the product. There, thermal underwear is almost a foreign product except for skiers. The difference in geography is a key element in developing a sound advertising strategy.

Next, define your target demographically. Demographics are those hard, cold, measurable facts, such as income, age, sex, car-ownership, number of children, married or single that are used to describe people. All these facts will assist you in developing a strong advertising strategy. For example, people who live in single-family houses have and need different things than those who live in apartments. Lawn equipment, hot water tanks, exterior paint, and liability insurance are common to home owners but not apartment dwellers. The same sort of example can be drawn for married persons with several children living in a house compared to single persons living alone in an apartment. Describe the demographics of your target market as completely as possible.

Psychographic descriptions come next on the list. Psychographics are non-measurable characteristics of your target's lifestyle. For example, a single male, age 23, living in a major city in an apartment may be a swinger who is interested in music, entertaining and social activities, spending practically no time at home.

Another male fitting the same demographic description may be a college student planning a career in medicine. He may spend a great deal of time in the apartment studying, almost never entertains, is primarily interested in holding down expenses to pay for his education, and is a gourmet cook.

Still another young man with the same demographics may be a blue-collar worker with little education who is interested in sports, watches much television, and primarily eats frozen dinners.

All are the same demographically, but they lead vastly different lives. This "lifestyle analysis" often defines your target as accurately as the more conventional demographic information.

Because you know your product, you should be able to describe fairly well the type of person to whom your product should appeal. You should be able to identify why and how your product might fit into his or her lifestyle or the benefits each person might receive over and above the purely physical properties the product offers.

After you determine the psychographics of the target, you need to identify the media he uses. Be careful here. The job is to identify the type of media your target uses, not the media in which you plan to place your advertising.

Let's look again at our example of the three young men. The first man, the swinger, might rely heavily on radio for his entertainment and practically never watch television. His reading habits might run to pop magazines such as *Rolling Stone, Heavy Metal,* and others. Our second young man also might be a heavy radio user but of a different type. He might listen only to classical stations. He might read newspapers a lot, watch primarily educational or scientific television programming, and subscribe to magazines that might help him in his interests such as *Psychology Today, Health,* or *Prevention.* Our third young man might be a heavy newspaper user, but read only the sports section. He might watch a great deal of television, but primarily sports events on the weekends and in prime time. He might listen to practically no radio, but subscribe to *Sports Illustrated, Sport* and other magazines which fit his interests.

Define the media used by your target. It can have a great deal to do with your advertising strategy.

Next, define how your *target* will purchase or use your product. Recall the types of customers described in the first part of this chapter. Where does your target fit?

If he has never heard of your product and is satisfied with what he is using, it will be a difficult task to get him to try your product. If, however, he is seeking the benefit you offer, or is looking for a solution to a problem your product will solve, the task will be easier.

For example, among the three young men described above, an electric Chinese wok would probably appeal to only one of the three, the gourmet cook. The other two would not be prospects. Similarly, probably only one of the three, the swinger, would be interested in purchasing the latest stereo speakers, promising the greatest sound ever.

Where your prospect shops or how he purchases your product is also important. One person might shop in the neighborhood grocery, another in a large supermarket chain, and still another in a gourmet food store. Since most products don't have 100 percent distribution in all types of outlets, the availability of your product to the prospect is a guiding factor in strategy development. Don't attempt to force people to change their shopping habits just to obtain your product. Find prospects who frequent the type of outlets where your product is available. Concentrate your efforts on them.

Step Three: The third step is the essence of your advertising strategy. It is the benefit or problem solution which you plan to offer to the person you have described as your target.

Your strategy can be based on a Unique Selling Proposition if you believe that to be the strongest approach. You might choose to go with a form of Brand Image, or you might find Positioning works best. The primary point is to select the single promise which will provide the strongest benefit or problem solution for the person you have described in Step Two. Then, translate that into a statement of advertising strategy.

Be sure to remember the four guides to a successful advertising strategy described in Chapter 4.

1. The strategy must offer a consumer benefit or solve a consumer problem.
2. The benefit offered or the solution promised must be wanted or desired by the consumer.
3. The brand must be tied directly to the benefit or problem solution offered.
4. The benefit or problem solution must be communicable through media advertising.

One good way to test the promise you plan to make your prospect is to think of yourself as a door-to-door salesperson. Assume you are going to sell your product or service in person. Would the promise you plan to make be something you would say if you were calling in person? Or, is your offer simply a group of words which you have strung together? Remember, advertising is selling. If you don't really have a sales message which will provide a benefit to the consumer or solve a consumer problem, would the person behind the door you knocked on listen to what you have to say? That's a good test of your sales message.

Here is where the real thinking must come in. There is no easy solution to developing a successful advertising strategy. But, if you know your product and know your target market, you should be able to generate an advertising strategy that has real appeal.

Step Four: Once you have developed your advertising strategy using either a USP, a Brand Image, or a Positioning statement, the next step is to develop the additional selling points that support your strategy. It's important the additional selling points *support* your advertising strategy, not detract from it because you are trying to include additional strategies in your sales message. Remember, your message must be single-minded. The additional selling points should support that strategy only. Don't drift into other areas.

Assume you're developing an advertising strategy for Cheer detergent. Your benefit is Cheer gets clothes clean in all water temperatures. Therefore it can be used for all types of fabrics. You might support this by listing the various types of fabrics which could be washed. You might list the advantages of using hot, warm, and cold water in the washing machine for various fabrics. You might show the savings of having only one detergent on hand. All these would support your "all temperature" strategy. You certainly wouldn't want to list an additional selling point such as Cheer contains special bleaching agents. That has nothing to do with your "all temperature" appeal. It only serves to confuse your consumer. Similarly, it's doubtful you'd want to stress something such as low sudsing. Again, that has nothing to do with your strategy.

Be sure your additional selling points support and reinforce your advertising strategy. Be single-minded and be sure your advertising strategy is single-minded also.

Step Five: The fifth step is to describe the technique you plan to use in presenting your advertising strategy. Technique simply means what method of presentation would best present your message. What tone do you want to employ with your message? For example, some strategies seem to call for a news technique such as an announcement. Others may be better suited to a conservative, factual approach. Still others need music. Much will depend on the type of message you have developed and the type of benefit you are offering.

While the technique often depends on the execution of your strategy, many times the strategy itself dictates the type of approach that should be used with the execution. Be sure your technique matches the message you're presenting.

Step Six: The final step in the development of an advertising strategy is to relate your strategy directly to the advertising objectives you have established. Remember the importance of communication effects. These were described in Chapters 2 and 3 as being the best way to measure advertising results. Describe exactly how your advertising strategy and its message will achieve your advertising objectives. Because most advertising objectives are a direct measure of the effect of the advertising message which comes from the advertising strategy, this simply ties your advertising package into a neat bundle.

Will these six steps to developing an advertising strategy work? Can you do it? Will the strategy be sound? Yes, up to a point. These steps won't help you think, but they will help channel your thinking. Nothing can take the place of sound ideas that are well expressed. That's what this outline is designed to do. If you use it properly, it can help you develop strong, effective advertising strategies.

Looking at an Example

Perhaps the best review of the development of an advertising strategy is an example. Below is an advertising strategy developed by a group of students. Note that it flows step-by-step to a logical conclusion.

**EXAMPLE OF AN
ADVERTISING STRATEGY FOR
ACME VEGETABLE YOGURT**

1. *Product definition.*

   This is the new Swiss-style vegetable yogurt from Acme. The product is made from natural yogurt cultures with fresh vegetable pieces mixed throughout. It makes a unique party dip.

2. *Defining "Susan"*

   A. Geographics.

   Susan lives in a house in Chestnut Hill, a suburb of Boston.

   B. Demographics.

   Susan is 30 years old, married and has a five-year-old son. She graduated from Boston University and now works as a free-lance photographer. Susan's husband is a lawyer, and their household income is $42,000 a year.

   C. Psychographics.

   Susan is an active woman. She is an innovator and likes to try new things. She and her husband are very busy with many social obligations. Dining out and party giving are important parts of Susan's life. She is concerned about keeping fit and so tries to eat healthful, natural foods.

D. Media patterns.

Susan watches about one hour each of daytime and primetime television per day. She also watches the 11 p.m. news and occasionally the "Tonight Show" or a late movie. Susan listens to AM radio in the morning while preparing for the day. She subscribes to *Cosmopolitan* and *Photography* magazines, and also occasionally reads *VIVA*. Susan subscribes to the *Boston Globe* newspaper and reads the *New York Times* twice a week. Susan is exposed to outdoor advertising as she spends time working and socializing in the city.

E. Buying/Use Patterns.

Susan is a heavy user of Acme fruit yogurt. She buys 10 to 12 cups of yogurt each week at a local supermarket. Susan eats the yogurt for lunch and her husband and son eat it for snacks and desserts. They all eat yogurt because they enjoy the taste and know it's good for them.

3. *Unique Selling Proposition.*

The product is a unique, natural vegetable yogurt dip from Acme. It is the only vegetable yogurt dip available. It will be called Acme Dip-It.

4. *Additional Selling Points.*

Acme Dip-it is available in three flavors — carrot, green bean, and garden salad.

5. *Technique.*

Acme Dip-it will be advertised on daytime, primetime and late fringe television. Local radio commercials will be run on weekday mornings. Magazine and newspaper advertising will also be important, and outdoor advertising will be used as well. It should be "newsy" and modern in tone.

6. *Advertising Objectives.*

The prime objective is to build awareness of Acme Dip-it as a new Swiss-style vegetable yogurt dip. We want to build the awareness of 65 per cent of the target market, and this will be measured by interviewing consumers to determine awareness and advertising recall levels.

Let's Test Your Strategy Development Ability

We've discussed advertising strategy in great detail. We've given you an outline of six steps to follow. Now, let's see if you can do it.

We'll start with a simple exercise.

Following is an advertisement for the North Texas Commission featuring the Dallas-Fort Worth Airport which opened a few years ago. It was physically the largest airport in the world at that time. The ad appeared in the *Wall Street Journal, Business Week, Fortune, Dun's Review, The New Yorker,* and *U.S. News & World Report,* among other magazines.

Using the advertisement and the strategy outline we have just discussed, write down what you think might have been the strategy from which this ad was developed. In other words, we're doing this in reverse. You can see the ad that resulted; can you work back to the strategy from which it came? (Hint: This ad was not designed to get people to come to the airport or to fly to Dallas-Fort Worth.)

FIGURE 6-1

Why Dallas/FortWorth needs an airport as big as Manhattan.

©NTC. 1977

Dallas/Fort Worth Airport is the largest in the nation. It's three times as big as Kennedy and larger than Manhattan. But we didn't build it just to be big.

We're going to need it. The Southwest Metroplex is the reason why. DFW has been built for the future. But in many ways, the future is here now. We need the airport because we're the fashion, financial, and manufacturing center for the

In the year 2000, it will still be big enough.

Southwest. We need the airport because of the large number of corporate headquarters here and because of the traffic they generate. Only New York and Chicago have more million dollar companies than Dallas/Fort Worth. (1,017 million-dollar companies now make their home here.)

An airport isn't the only reason to consider Dallas/Fort Worth.

We'd hope that the largest airport in America would be a factor, yes. But there are many good reasons for considering Dallas/Fort Worth as the future home for your company. We have a work force of over a million; over 40,000 acres of industrial parks; and new Class A office space for as little as $7 per square foot.

The quality of life is high and the cost of living is low.

The cost of living is 12% lower than the national metropolitan average. Taxes are 32% below the national average. Housing costs are lowest among the 10 largest metro areas. And with more house, you get our excellent area schools, friendly neighbors and, in most cases, an easy commute. (The average commute in the Metroplex is twenty minutes.)

In Dallas/Fort Worth, there's plenty to do too. There are 31 lakes within 100 miles; 75 municipal pools; hundreds of lighted tennis courts; and 60 golf courses playable 12 months a year. There's rodeo, professional sports,

and America's largest state fair. There are 47 colleges and universities, along with art galleries, opera, and some of the best theatre west of New York.

America's largest airport is just one reason to consider Dallas/Fort Worth. We think when you consider all of them, you'll see why more and more businesses are moving here. Because Dallas/Fort Worth offers your company a place to grow and prosper along with a great environment for your family. It's the sensible alternative.

Clip this coupon and find out more.

If you are considering moving your company to Dallas/Fort Worth, you're bound to have questions. You'll find the answers in the Businessman's Inventory. It's yours for the asking. Just clip the coupon below and send it on.

A Businessman's Inventory of Dallas Fort Worth The Southwest Metroplex 1977

The Businessman's Inventory contains information on economic rankings, office space and industrial parks, labor and tax structure, and much more. Send for it now.
Mr. Jack O'Callaghan, President North Texas Commission P.O. Box 61246 Dallas/Fort Worth Airport, Texas 75261

| NAME |
| TITLE |
| COMPANY |
| ADDRESS |
| CITY | STATE | ZIP |

The North Texas Commission is a non-profit, regional marketing organization supported by the businesses and local governments of the Dallas/Fort Worth SMSA.

Dallas/FortWorth: The Southwest Metroplex.

The Sensible Alternative

Essentials of Advertising Strategy

An Assignment

NAME ————————————

Course ————————————

Date ————————————

1. What is the product or service North Texas Commission is trying to promote?
   (Define your product or service)

2. Who is the target market North Texas Commission is trying to reach?
   (Define target market)

    A. Where does the TM work or live?
   (Geographics)

    B. What are their demographic characteristics?
   (Demographics)

C. What are their psychographic characteristics?
   (Psychographics)

D. What media does the TM use?
   (Media patterns)

E. How would the TM buy or use the product or service North Texas Commission is promoting?
   (Buying/Use Patterns)

3. What is the message North Texas Commission is trying to communicate to the TM?
   (USP/Positioning/Identity)

4. What additional selling points support the main sales message?
   (Additional selling points)

5. What technique did North Texas Commission use to get their message to the TM?
   (Technique)

6. What advertising objectives do you think North Texas Commission set for this ad?
   (Define advertising objectives)

Do advertising strategies work? You bet they do. Here are just a few examples of outstanding advertising strategies from the past. Look at each advertisement. Jot down the strategy from which the advertisement was developed. See if you can get a picture of the target market to which the strategy was directed.

SFX: Trumpets

TOURNAMENT MASTER: "Marvelous joust Sir Avery. Refreshments for the victor!"

V.O.: "When it comes to great cheese flavor."

AVERY: "Cheese!"

V.O.: "There's one snack that will win your heart."

"Nacho cheese flavored Doritos brand tortilla chips."

SFX: CRUNCH!

SFX: Armour falling off.

GIRL: Giggles.

V.O.: "So for a snack with the great flavor of..."

AVERY: "Cheese!"

V.O. "Try Nacho Cheese Doritos. They taste as good as they crunch."

FIGURE 6-2. Doritos, a tortilla chip made from corn, was a product that was not widely known in the early 1960's. Based on a strategy of offering the chip with the most "crunch," Doritos is now the leading snack food in the country. The consumer wants a "crunchy" chip. Doritos strategy speaks directly to that desire.

HERO: (SUNG) Oh
no, not for me, Sir.

I need originality, Sir.

Give me innovation,
variation, Dr Pepper ...

It's not a cola.

It's something much, much
more.

It's not a root beer.

HERO & GROUP: (SUNG)
Drink Dr Pepper!

The joy of every boy and
girl.

It's the most original soft
drink ever

FIGURE 6-3. Dr Pepper was a product with a problem. People didn't know what flavor to expect. By developing an advertising strategy as "The world's most misunderstood soft drink," Dr Pepper was able to explain that it "wasn't a cola, not a root beer, but something much, much more." It was the "most unusual soft drink in the whole wide world." This strategy has been continued and expanded over the years. The benefit: A new and unusual soft drink taste for the consumer.

Does she...or doesn't she?

Hair color so natural only her hairdresser knows for sure!

She's as full of fun as a kid—and just as fresh looking. And this is a lovely thing in a mother! But staying young is not only thinking young, it's *looking* young too. And here, the fresh, young, even color you get *every time* with Miss Clairol, makes the beautiful difference. It's like discovering how to turn back time. It certainly is the best way to keep gray from ever showing.

Keeps hair in wonderful condition—soft, silky. Because Miss Clairol carries color deep into the hair strand, it shines outward with a clear, all-over even tone the way natural color does. That's why hairdressers everywhere recommend Miss Clairol and more women use it than any other haircoloring. So quick and easy. Try it yourself. Today. **MISS CLAIROL**

Even close up, her hair looks natural. Miss Clairol keeps it shiny, bouncy. Completely covers gray with the younger, brighter lasting color no other kind of haircoloring can promise—and live up to!

HAIR COLOR BATH is a trademark of Clairol Inc. © Clairol Inc. 1964

FIGURE 6-4. Clairol hair coloring startled the country in the early 1960's with the statement "Does she or doesn't she? Only her hair dresser knows for sure." The consumer benefit: Here was a hair coloring so natural only the person who applied it knew for sure. A bit shocking for the time but a strategy that has lived on for years.

Back when the business world was dominated by men, some women carried a lot of weight around the office.

You've come a long way, baby.

VIRGINIA SLIMS

Slimmer than the fat cigarettes men smoke.

Fashions: Richard Assatly

16 mg "tar," 0.9 mg nicotine av. per cigarette, FTC Report Aug. '77

Warning: The Surgeon General Has Determined That Cigarette Smoking Is Dangerous to Your Health.

FIGURE 6-5. Virginia Slims cigarettes caught onto the evolving women's liberation movement with the line "You've come a long way, baby" to express its strategy. The benefit: A cigarette just for women, especially the modern woman. In addition, the strategy has offered widespread promotional opportunities for the brand in premiums, sports events, and other areas.

Soft Whiskey.
Is it hard liquor?

Soft Whiskey is hard liquor that isn't "hard."

It doesn't have a "hard" edge to sting-bite-burn you on the way down. Incidentally, one of the ways we make it Soft is by doing some of our distilling in small batches instead of large ones. (To protect all our hard work, we can't tell you the other ways.)

Make no mistake about it, Calvert Extra is as whiskey a whiskey as any whiskey you can buy. It does anything "hard" liquor can do.

But does it softer.

Soft Whiskey swallows easy—with warmth, not heat. In your mixed drinks, it doesn't fight the mixer.

It blends smoothly, but doesn't lose itself. Even melting rocks can't cut the richness of its flavor. (You might call 86 proof Calvert Extra the ideal whiskey.)

Distillers have been pipe-dreaming Soft Whiskey for years. But until recently nobody's been able to produce it. At our distillery alone, there were more than 22,000 unsuccessful Soft Whiskey experiments. (As you can see, anyone else who tries to reproduce Soft Whiskey has his work cut out for him.)

Before you sample Calvert Extra, the Soft Whiskey, there's something you ought to know: you may never touch a drop of "hard" liquor again.

BLENDED WHISKEY · 86 PROOF · 65% GRAIN NEUTRAL SPIRITS · CALVERT DIST. CO., LOUISVILLE, KY.

FIGURE 6-6. Hard liquor. Soft whiskey? The Calvert strategy took the entire liquor category by surprise. Traditionally, liquor advertising had spoken of smoothness, taste, proof, etc., but never "softness." A new product developed to fit the strategy helped move the brand up in the marketplace.

Chapter 7
From Strategy To Execution

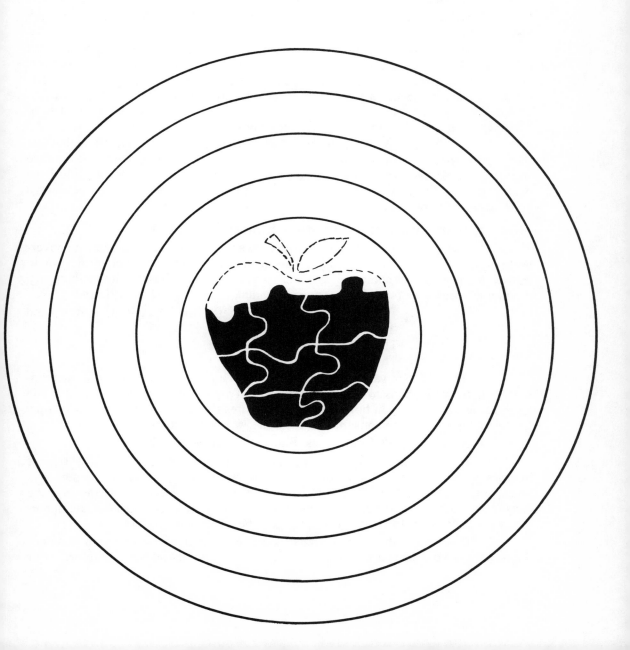

In the introduction, you recall, we said this wasn't a book on copywriting. However, to understand the creative aspect of advertising some attention must be given to writing advertisements or commercials. The next few chapters will give an overview of that area. The viewpoint, however, will be evaluative rather than developmental.

From Strategy to Execution

Once the advertising strategy has been developed, the job of developing an ad is well underway. The next step is the execution. Referring again to our definition in Chapter 1, an advertising execution is:

"The physical form in terms of art, illustration, copy, music, etc., in which the advertising strategy is presented to the target market."

In other words, the "what" of the message must be translated into the "how" form of presentation. You know what you want to say. Now, how do you go about saying it?

Because we have built such a strong case for the advertising strategy, you might be asking is the execution all that important? The answer, without hesitation, is yes. A brilliant execution can make a mediocre strategy into a winner. On the other hand, a mediocre execution can greatly reduce the effectiveness of a brilliant strategy. The best of all worlds is a strong strategy with an exciting execution. But what is an exciting execution? Perhaps some examples will help.

All six examples are built on sound advertising strategies. The thing that sets them apart from the crowd, however, is the execution, the way in which the creative strategy is presented. There are probably many other ways each strategy could have been executed. But it was the creative approach that made the difference between a good advertisement and a great one.

How Do You Translate a Strategy into an Execution?

Every person who has ever written an advertisement or translated an advertising strategy into an execution has a plan for doing the job, a formula or a "way to think." Many examples could be given. Perhaps the best though is the simple three step method advocated by one of the country's leading package good advertisers.

1. The copy must present a benefit which the consumer wants and the product can deliver.
2. The words have to be good.
3. The pictures have to be good.

That's it. Not very exciting but it works. Once you have picked out the product's benefit, your job is to find the words to tell your story in a clear, dramatic and memorable way. Then you have to find the pictures that go with the words which tell the benefit you want the consumer to associate with your product.

Sound simple? Sure it does. But it ain't necessarily so.

In translating a strategy into an execution, your primary job is that of interpreter. You interpret what the advertiser wants to say to his customers and prospects. You're the conduit. The words and pictures you select are the message the consumer will receive. If you pick poor words or weak pictures, you limit the opportunity for consumers to receive the message. The advertising suffers.

One way to think about translating executions is to assume your audience doesn't speak your language. They can't understand a word you say. Therefore, your presentation has to be graphically clear so the message comes across in an instant. It can't require an explanation or the "what we mean by that is . . . " which seems so prevalent in advertising today. Your translation should be crystal clear to everyone, especially your target market.

The "Big Idea"

Most successful advertising executions are built around a "big idea" — an idea so strong that it is instantly accepted. It should make the reader or viewer say "I never thought of it that way" or "Gee, that really sounds good. I need one." While the "big idea" is hard to explain, it's easy to recognize. It's the advertising that makes you stop, think, and remember. Here are some excellent examples of "big ideas."

Many times, you'll find a "big idea" is based on the unexpected. It's uncommon. It's a different way of looking at something. For example, when all the other automakers were describing how long, low, big, and beautiful their automobiles were, Volkswagen was telling how small and efficient its "Bug" was. This was a unique presentation of an outstanding strategy. VW could have shown their car in a large, overwhelming way. However, its choice of execution and words got the message across better than anything else they could have done.

4. Five cars.

5. Five dead batteries.

6. But we're going to start all five, all at once, . . .

7. . . .with one battery, . . .

8. . . .a two year old Sears DieHard Battery.

9. (Sfx: engines starting) The DieHard.

FIGURE 7-1. The strategy for the Sears Die Hard battery is quite clear. It offers the consumer the benefit of a long-lasting automobile battery. Nearly all batteries make that same claim in one way or another. The difference in Sears claim is the execution. This storyboard illustrates how the execution not only carries out the strategy but even extends it in a most memorable way.

BENNY GOODMAN: Restaurants and night clubs.

GEORGE GALLUP: I use it for business traveling and entertaining.

WILLIAM MILLER: In Tokoyo, Paris and upstate New York.

CHARLES CONRAD: Why, someday I may even use it on the moon.

SAM ERVIN: With this, maybe they'll treat me like somebody important.

JACK GILFORD: Even if they don't know this adorable face.

ANNCR (VO): To apply for an American Express Card, call 800-528-8000, . . .

or look for this display wherever the Card is welcomed.

BARBARA FELDON: The American Express Card.

JACK NICKLAUS: Don't leave home without it.

MUPPETS: Don't leave home without it.

(MUSICAL TAG)
MEL BLANC: Tha-tha- that's all folks.

FIGURE 7-2. This campaign for American Express, "Do You Know Me?", has won many awards. The strategy again is simple. People may not know *you* but they know the American Express credit card. The unique approach of using well-known names but relatively unknown faces helps put across the benefits of the American Express card vividly and clearly.

1. (SILENT)

2. (SFX: TRUCK'S HORN)

3. (SFX: TRUCK)

5. (SFX) ANNCR: (VO) American Tourister would like to remind you

6. (SFX) that the reason we make our suitcases so strong

7. (SFX) isn't just to protect our suitcases.

9. what's inside our suitcases.

10. (SFX: EGG CRACKING)

11. (SILENT)

FIGURE 7-3. American Tourister's luggage strategy is to show that its luggage stands up under all kinds of travel conditions. This is the same strategy most luggage manufacturers probably try to employ. The difference is the execution. Showing a truck hitting an American Tourister suitcase and then the surprise of the egg does the trick.

3. Last year, the Abbot asked me to do an impossible job—

4. (RIPPLE DISSOLVE TO OLD COMMERCIAL)

5. copy 500 sets of this manuscript.

9. to save paper, he wants it copied on both sides. And he wants it fast.

10. This is going to take another miracle!

11. (MUSIC)

15. It automatically copies on both sides . . .

16. of the same sheet of paper . . .

17. at the incredible speed of two pages a second.

FIGURE 7-4. Xerox makes copying machines. So do several other companies. But how do you get the idea of true reproduction across? Through one of the most well-remembered commercials of all time, "Brother Dominic" for Xerox. The strategy is simple, the execution brilliant.

1. JESS: Pretty boy! Pretty boy!

2. PARROT: Pretty boy! (Screech) Pretty boy!

3. JESS: Every Maytag Repairman should have a nice pet like you. PARROT: (Squawk)

4. JESS: (Big sigh) Kinda takes my mind off of being lonely.

5. PARROT: Lonely! Lonely!

6. JESS: (Wistful) You see, it's these Maytag Washers...

7. ...they're really built. (Sfx: solid thunk)

8. JESS: (Helplessly) They're so darn dependable.

9. PARROT: Dependable! Dependable!

10. JESS: (Wistfully) You can say that again.

11. PARROT: Dependable! Dependable!

12. JESS: (Mildly) Alright do you have to rub it in????

FIGURE 7-5. Maytag appliances are dependable. That strategy has been executed in several ways. But the execution that really gets the idea across is the "Lonely Repairman." What better way to say Maytags are dependable than by showing the repairman who never gets a call. A sound strategy. A truly exciting execution.

ANNCR: (VO) In Soviet Georgia,

there are two curious things about the people.

A large part of their diet is yogurt. And a large number of them live past 100.

Of course, many things affect longevity,

and we're not saying Dannon Yogurt will help you live longer.

But Dannon is a natural, wholesome food that does supply many nutrients.

By the way, 89-year-old Bagrat Topagua

liked Dannon so much, he ate two cups.

That pleased his mother very much.

FIGURE 7-6. The Dannon strategy was to demonstrate the healthful qualities of yogurt and show that Dannon is the leader. The execution? Film the commercials in Soviet Georgia where people eat lots of yogurt and live well over 100 years. The result? An execution that sets Dannon head and shoulders above competitors.

BUBBA SMITH: I had my own way of tackling.

I used to grab the whole backfield.

Then I threw the guys out until I found the one with the ball.

When I started drinking beer,

I did the same thing, and this is the one I'm holding on to.

Lite Beer from Miller.

It has a third less calories than their regular beer.

It's less filling and it tastes terrific too.

(SFX: RRRPPP)

I also love the easy openin' can.

ANNCR: (VO) Lite Beer from Miller. Everything you always wanted in a beer.

And less.

FIGURE 7-7. The use of sports heroes in beer advertising isn't a new idea. The idea of using former sports heroes is. The Miller strategy is strong: "Less filling. Great Taste." But it's the execution that really gets the message across, as Bubba Smith demonstrates in this commercial.

ANNCR: (VO) Incredible... The hundreds of blood vessels in your eyes

can swell to three, (SFX)

even four times (SFX) their normal size, when your eyes are tired, burning, itching.

For relief of minor eye irritation, use Visine.

In seconds

Visine shrinks swollen blood vessels

down (SFX), down (SFX),

down (SFX) to normal again.

Now they're soothed, relieved, they feel great.

And there's no more red, so they look great.

For tired, irritated eyes... Visine (SFX PING) gets the red out.

FIGURE 7-8. A catchy phrase, "Gets the red out," translates into a "big idea" for Visine. A demonstration tells the story. Visine used the same commercial for two years without change. "Big ideas" last.

FIGURE 7-9. The "big idea" for Kool-Aid is graphic, the "Smiling Pitcher." Kids and adults alike know and recognize the brand based on this "big idea". Kool-Aid is fun. Now, Kool-Aid even uses the "Smiling Pitcher" on the package.

Think small.

Our little car isn't so much of a novelty any more.

A couple of dozen college kids don't try to squeeze inside it.

The guy at the gas station doesn't ask where the gas goes.

Nobody even stares at our shape.

In fact, some people who drive our little flivver don't even think that about 27 miles to the gallon is going any great guns.

Or using 5 pints of oil instead of 5 quarts.

Or never needing anti-freeze.

Or racking up about 40,000 miles on a set of tires.

That's because once you get used to some of our economies, you don't even think about them any more.

Except when you squeeze into a small parking spot. Or renew your small insurance. Or pay a small repair bill. Or trade in your old VW for a new one.

Think it over.

Dealer Name

FIGURE 7-10. This advertisement for Volkswagen was chosen as the top advertisement of the past 100 years in a poll conducted by *Advertising Age* in 1976. It's a brilliant strategy, a great execution, and a truly "big idea" all rolled into one.

But, Can You Learn to be Creative?

That question has been argued as long as there has been advertising. Many people believe the ability to do creative advertising is a gift, a talent that can't be taught. It's innate. Others say creativity can be taught, that it can be learned like any other subject.

It's probably true that some people are naturally better at synthesizing ideas, at finding different combinations of words and pictures or at looking at things in a different way, just as there are people who are better at playing the trombone than others. Generally, though, most people have a built-in creative ability. It's just a question of harnessing it or learning to use it.

James Webb Young, a former creative executive at J. Walter Thompson Co. advertising agency, believed anyone could be creative or could be taught to be creative. He developed a series of steps called "A Technique for Producing Ideas," which has been used for more than 30 years.[1] In condensed form, here's what Young suggested:

> "This is the whole process or method by which ideas are produced: First, the gathering of raw materials — both the materials of your immediate problem and the materials which come from a constant enrichment of your store of general knowledge. Second, the working over of these materials in your mind. Third, the incubating state where you let something beside the conscious mind do the work of synthesis. Fourth, the actual birth of the idea — the 'Eureka! I have it!' stage. And fifth, the final shaping and development of the idea to practical usefulness."

While Young makes it appear that almost anyone can create advertising ideas, the task is usually more difficult. One major hindrance to creativity is that not enough information about the product has been gathered. If the mind is full of information about the situation and the problem to be solved by the product, a solution usually will emerge, and then this solution can be developed into advertisements or executions. Perhaps a more specific "how to" list will help the inexperienced. First, we'll look at some specific suggestions on data gathering. Then we'll investigate how some advertising experts suggest developing sound advertising ideas.

How to Develop Executions

While there is no magic formula guaranteeing success in translating an advertising strategy into a magnificent execution, there are some common steps which may help in the process. These steps not only aid in understanding the translation of strategies into executions, but they will be helpful in evaluating the work of others.

1. *Understand the level of sale.*

   Very simply that means in order to develop a strong execution, you have to know what level of mental attitude your execution must effect. In other words, how strongly does the prospect feel about your product or service, the benefit you offer, or the problem solution you propose? Experts in consumer behavior have broken down most judgment feelings into three levels — opinions, attitudes, and beliefs. These are on an ascending scale in terms of importance to the person.

Opinions usually are judgments that are important only at the moment. For example, we form an opinion about a television show we saw last night, or a dress we saw in a store window, or a food we had in a restaurant. We have some sort of opinion about almost everything around us.

A more lasting judgment usually is formed about other things such as products we use on a regular basis or whether we like football or a particular person. These are called attitudes. Attitudes usually are based on longer term experiences.

Judgments that are very important to us are called beliefs. These are things that are basic to our lives such as our religion, our country, our work, etc.

It is the strength of a consumer's judgment that will set the tone of the advertising execution. For example, if we are trying to influence an opinion, only a simple presentation might be needed. To persuade someone to try a new flavor of chewing gum shouldn't require a long involved presentation of the various merits of the flavor compared to other flavors.

However, to influence an attitude would probably require more information and a different type of presentation and execution. To persuade a consumer to change brands of detergent or to start using a new type of product requires a more complete presentation of all the facts.

To change a belief, the execution of the message can become quite involved. For example, to persuade a person to change religions is serious business. It would likely require much information, support, and rationale.

2. *Develop an appeal.*

What makes people react? Some psychologists have suggested there are three basic human needs: Hunger, thirst, and sex. Others have suggested we react based on our emotions of love, hate, fear, and anger. Still others have suggested there are a multitude of factors, some listing as many as 24 things that can influence behavior. Whatever the number, we know there are certain appeals to which people react. Some have greater strength than others in motivating people.

While the following list is certainly not inclusive, it does give an indication of the types of appeals that can be used in advertising executions.

   A. To be popular, attractive, wanted
   B. To have physical things
   C. To enjoy life through comfort or convenience
   D. To create a happy family situation
   E. To have power

    F. To avoid fear

    G. To have love and sex

    H. To emmulate others

    I. To have new experiences, feelings, sensory effects

    J. To protect or maintain health

Each execution must have some sort of appeal to the prospect. Identifying the most important appeal in the strategy often helps develop the execution. An appeal to one of the prospect's basic needs or desires can help make the ad stand out more than others.

3. *Empathize with the prospect*

A strong execution often has thorough empathy with the prospect. By empathy we mean knowing and understanding how the consumer feels about your product or service. For example, it is important to know how much information the consumer has about your product or service. Using an execution that assumes the consumer knows too much leaves him behind. A prospect won't work to learn something from an advertisement. You must present all the information he needs in a simple, easy-to-understand way. That requires empathy or understanding what he knows or wants to know.

Similarly, you must have some understanding about how the prospect feels about your product. If you put yourself in the place of the prospect, it helps greatly. Can you imagine what it would be like to be a 68-year-old man living alone? What would it be like to be a mother of nine children? If you were living in Montana, how would you feel about cowboy boots?

Empathy is understanding how prospects feel. Get outside of yourself. Go where your prospects are. The better you project yourself into your prospect's situation, lifestyle, feelings, etc., the stronger the execution you can develop.

4. *Build a story.*

Your advertising must be like a classic drama, i.e., it must have a beginning, a middle, and an end. Don't start in the middle and expect people to know where you are. Have a logical flow of ideas or events. Build toward a climax. Your message must make sense. It must flow. Again, people are too busy to have to work to understand your message. Make it simple. Make it easy to understand. Make it worthwhile for the consumer. Everyone likes a story, particularly when it is about or involves them.

Also remember that as a storyteller and interpreter, you must speak the language of your audience. People are not impressed with glowing literary phrases. Most consumers don't know a noun from a gerund or care. Write the way you talk or the way your prospects talk. Don't try to impress readers with your mastery of the obtuse phrase. Use common, everyday words they know and can understand. Your purpose in an execution is to communicate, not to impress.

5. *Don't let the execution overwhelm the message.*

    Too many times, advertisements are remembered only for the execution. That is, you remember the cute idea, the clever words, the pretty scene but can't recall the message or the advertiser. Advertising should entertain but not so much that it interferes with the sales message. Remember, the execution is simply the way you get your message across; it's not a goal in itself. If the advertisement or commercial is remembered and the sales message forgotten, then that ad is a failure. Getting the sales message through to the prospect should always be uppermost in your mind. That's the purpose of advertising.

6. *Ask for the order.*

    Even though we have said in several places that advertising can't be expected to do the complete selling job, always try to finish the sale. Too often advertisements lead the prospect right up to the point of purchase and then stop. The advertiser seems embarrassed to ask for the order, to attempt to complete the sale.

    Advertising is a form of selling. A good salesman always asks for the order and so should your advertising. Each advertisement or commercial should be a complete sales message and that includes some way of encouraging the reader or viewer to do something. Don't wait. Ask for the order in every advertisement.

    Will these "rules" ensure a successful execution? Probably not, but if you include each of them in every advertisement, they do assure that a sound advertising message has been developed.

Chapter 8
What Do The Experts Say?

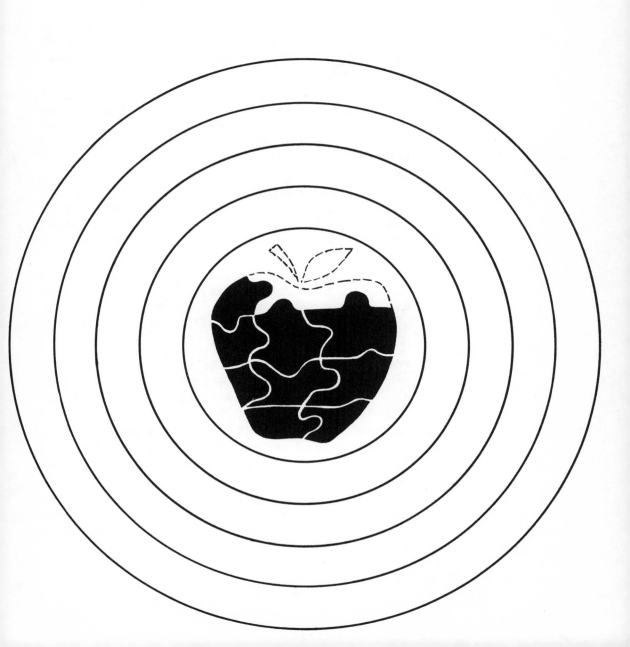

Only a few extremely successful creative people in advertising have taken the time to give others the complete details of how to create great advertising. Most of these suggestions have been offered through speeches or writings. Below is a sampling of comments made by some of the current recognized authorities.

Doyle Dane Bernbach

Bill Bernbach, one of the founders of the agency that created memorable campaigns for clients such as Volkswagen, Avis, Polaroid, Clairol, Coast soap, Chevis Regal scotch whiskey, and American Tourister, had this to say:

1. Make your people and products close and real . . . not just a picture of something but the actual thing. This will give a lifelike effect and, therefore, gain greater believability.

2. Go to the essence of the product. Advertising's flight from merchandise must be halted. State the product's essence in the simplest terms of its basic advantage. And state this both tangibly and memorably.

3. Where possible, make your merchandise an actor in the scene, not just a prop. This makes for a tremendously effective method of getting your product remembered — because the provocative element in your advertising is also the element that sells your product. This is so simply stated — so difficult to execute!

4. Merchandise, artfully presented, has inherent interest. It can often be, and often should be, the *very device* that attracts attention. People are materialistic. They like nice things. Make yours look so good they'll want to own it. It's not necessary to inject a baby or dogs to get attention — not even a pair of crossed nylons!

5. Be sure that the advertisement has a physical focal center — one big area that dominates, instead of many small areas that divide an ad up equally — and equally repels reading.

6. This total concept applies both to print and to television advertising.

7. We insist that copy and art must be fully integrated. They must be conceived as a unit — developed as a unit. We have no problems here of which comes first — copy or art. They both come simultaneously in our workshop.

8. We insist on advertising with vitality, with exuberance. This is the vague thing called "personality." When advertising has a personality — it is persuasively different; and it is the one because it is the other. We fight for bounce in our advertising.

9. It is little less than useless to employ a so-called gimmick in advertising — unless the gimmick, itself, tells the product story. The device that attracts attention must also tell the product story."[1]

Leo Burnett USA

Leo Burnett, founder of Leo Burnett USA, one of the country's largest advertising agencies, once explained "How *Not* To Write Advertising Copy." The Burnett agency has created outstanding advertising campaigns for Green Giant vegetables, Kellogg cereals, Star-Kist tuna, Keebler cookies, Cheer detergent, and others. Here's what Burnett had to say and the examples he used of poor advertising copy:

1. Dull recital of self-evident facts.

   If you want the best in peas, you want Green Giant. Green Giant peas are carefully grown and packed to assure you of ultimate flavor satisfaction. These big tender peas are the best-selling peas in America because they are best liked. Get some from your grocer today.

2. Highfalutin' rhapsody or plain bombast.

   The big green jewel of the vegetable kingdom. You never knew a pea could be like this — dewy-sweet, June-morning fresh, and overflowing with full pea flavor. This is no ordinary pea. This is a Green Giant pea, the big green jewel of the vegetable kingdom. Serve it with pride on a candlelit table and don't be surprised if your husband holds your hand a little tighter.

3. Demonstration of writer's cleverness with words.

   The peas plan that ends vegetable wars forever. The Green Giant, who is just about as big as a corn and pea man can get, has a plan that guarantees peas on earth forever — peas on earth, good will towards men. According to his plan, you just reach for a can of plump Green Giant peas. They're so sweet and tender that the worst vegetable hater in the family will surrender and nobody will call it a-peas-ment. Get some from your good old grocer, like now.

   "The really good writer will take a second and third look at everything he writes. He will ask himself such questions as these: (a) Does this copy track from first sentence to last; (b) Is there any irrelevant or repetitious garbage that could come out; (c) Is this merely a good piece of writing, or will it help make a sale; (d) Is there anything here that sounds like hogwash; (e) If I were on the other end of this piece of copy, would I believe it and act on it?

   "Good copy will take the reader/listener/viewer by the hand, leading him without a single misstep to an inescapable conclusion. (If you think you are in literature rather than selling, you're in the wrong business!)"[2]

Foote, Cone and Belding, Inc.

Over the years, this agency has created great advertising for Raid insect killer, Sears DieHard battery, Hallmark greeting cards, and Sherwin-Williams paints, to mention a few. Fairfax M. Cone, former chairman of the agency, had this to say:

"The Plain, Short Story of Good Advertising.

"Advertising is the business, or the art, if you please, of telling someone something that should be important to him. It is a substitute for talking to someone.

"It is the primary requirement of advertising to be clear, clear as to exactly what the proposition is.

"If it isn't clear, and clear at a glance or a whisper, very few people will take the time or the effort to try to figure it out.

"The second essential of advertising is that what must be clear must also be important. The proposition must have value.

"Third, the proposition (the promise) that is both clear and important must also have personal appeal. It should be beamed at its logical prospects; no one else matters.

"Fourth, the distinction in good advertising expresses the personality of the advertisers, for a promise is only as good as its maker.

"Finally, a good advertisement demands action. It asks for an order, or it exacts a mental pledge.

"Altogether these things define a desirable advertisement as one that will command attention but never be offensive.

"It will be reasonable, but never dull.

"It will be original, but never self-conscious.

"It will be imaginative, but never misleading.

"And because of what it is and what it is not, a properly prepared advertisement will always be convincing and it will make people act."[3]

Ogilvy & Mather

The Ogilvy & Mather agency has developed memorable advertising campaigns for American Express, Maxwell House, Merrill Lynch, Shell, Pepperidge Farm, and other clients. David Ogilvy, the founder, outlined his agency's success with "37 Precepts for Ad Writing" which he separates into guiding principles, copy, headline, and illustration:

37 PRECEPTS FOR AD WRITING
Principles

1. Before we create a new campaign, we study the product, the precedents, and the research.
2. *Content* is more important than form. *What* you say in advertising is more important than *how* you say it.
3. Unless your campaign is built around a big idea, it will pass like a ship in the night.
4. Every advertisement must be relevant to the copy platform, and must deliver the *basic selling theme* loud and clear.
5. The brand name must be visible at a glance. Almost all advertisements are deficient in brand identification.
6. Advertisements should be friendly, because people don't buy from salesmen who are bad-mannered.
7. It pays to give your brand a first-class ticket through life. People don't like to be seen consuming products which their friends regard as sleazy and third-class.
8. The consumer is not a moron. She is your wife. Don't insult her intelligence.

9. We must make our ads contemporary. The consumer is *younger than we are.*

10. We cannot *bore* people into buying our product. We can only interest them in buying it.

11. When you are lucky enough to get a great ad, repeat it. No great campaign has ever been continued too long, and no great advertisement has been repeated too often.

12. No committee can create anything.

Headlines

13. Headlines should appeal to the reader's self interest by promising a benefit.

14. Inject the maximum news into the headline. Products, like people, are most interesting when they are first born.

15. Include the brand name in the headline.

16. Write headlines which will induce the reader to read the subhead and the body copy. You cannot save souls in an empty church.

17. Write headlines which will sell. Don't worry about the *length* — 12- word headlines get almost as much readership as three-word headlines.

18. Never use a headline which requires readership of body copy to make it comprehensible.

19. Never use tricky or irrelevant headlines. Don't try to be clever. People read too fast to figure out what you are trying to say.

Copy

20. Don't expect people to read leisurely essays — no belles lettres.

21. Go straight to the point — don't beat about the bush.

22. Avoid superlatives, generalizations, platitudes.

23. Avoid analogies — "just as, so too." People don't bother with them.

24. Be specific and factual.

25. Be personal, enthusiastic, memorable — as if the reader were sitting next to you at dinner.

26. The average woman reads only four ads in the average issue of an average magazine. If you want your ad to be one of the four, you had better write interesting copy.

27. Tell the truth, but make the truth interesting.

28. Write sentences of less than 12 words.

29. Use at least 14 references to people per hundred words.

30. Use testimonials.

31. Give the reader helpful information in return for her time and attention.

32. Don't be afraid to write long copy — if necessary.

33. Put captions under all your illustrations and make them pregnant with brand name and sell.

Illustrations

34. Illustrations, like copy, should portray reward.
35. To attract women, show babies or women. To attract men, show men.
36. Put "story appeal" in all illustrations.
37. Always use photographs, never use art work. Photographs invariably attract more readers and sell more merchandise.[4]

Batten, Barton, Durstine & Osborn, Inc.

BBDO has created tremendously successful advertising campaigns for clients such as Dodge automobiles, Campbell soup, Gillette TRAC II, Hawaiian Punch, and Pepsi-Cola plus many others. In his book, "Me and Other Advertising Geniuses," Charlie Brower, former president and chief executive officer of BBDO, makes the following suggestions on what turns people off about advertising and what turns people on:

What Turns People Off to Advertising

1. Talking like a pitchman instead of like a friend.
2. Not knowing when to shut up.
3. Using too many sales points so they remember none.
4. Talking about the product instead of what it will do for the reader or listener.
5. Being too important about a product of small importance.
6. Being too urgent . . . too Hurry! Hurry! Hurry!
7. Making unbelievable and unsupported claims.
8. Being confusing.
9. Making the reader or listener work to get your message.
10. Being just plain silly.
11. Worst of all — being dull.

People are Turned on to Your Advertising by:

1. Friendly help — but not too friendly. Nobody wants you to wag your tail or jump up to lick his hand.
2. Simplicity (consider that as written ten times over).
3. Wit, but not clowning.
4. Real news, but not fake news.
5. Advertisements that reward reading or listening.
6. A logical development of a single idea.
7. Service suggestions (how to use).
8. New uses for familiar products.
9. Interest, even borrowed interest.

Brower also said, "It seems to me that the advertiser when he asks someone to read his advertisement or listen to his commercial, agrees to an unwritten contract: 'If you will spend part of your life with me, even though it be but a few seconds, I in turn will reward you. I will send you away with some bit of new information, however small, some degree of entertainment, be it ever so slight, some feeling of satisfaction that you did not have before.' "[5]

What if You Get Stuck?

Having followed all the rules, suggestions and ideas we have presented and the recommendations of the recognized advertising authorities, what happens if you still get stuck, if you can't find a great way to execute your strategy? What if the ideas just don't come?

Over the years, one approach has been to try to look at things in a different way. If you'll recall, in Chapter 7 we said the "big idea" often comes from the unexpected or from a different way of looking at the subject. Below is a list of different ways to approach a subject. Often, doing this sort of thing will help get the "creative juices" flowing again.

The Search for Different Ways of Looking at Things

1. Pick out the dominating idea. Avoid it. Distort it.
2. What are some interesting wrong ways to do it?
3. How would I describe it to someone who can't see it?
4. How can I visualize the problem? in 3-D? in 4-D?
5. Look at the problem from a different viewpoint.
6. Turn things upside down by consciously reversing some relationship.
7. Transfer the situation by analogy to another, more easily handled situation. (Adapt on copy.)
8. Deliberately shift emphasis from one part to another.
9. Expose yourself to a multitude of stimulations (supermarket, paper, pens, blocks, etc.).
10. Look at objects and try to develop ideas from them.
11. What is the *least* likely thing to happen?
12. How would a madman do it?
13. What if it went faster? Slower?
14. How might we do it if we did not have an investment of effort, inertia, commitment?
15. What are the forces acting on it? Increase them. Decrease them. Emphasize each.
16. What's a funny way to do it?
17. Ask why is it necessary?
18. Ask where should it be done?
19. When should it be done?
20. Who should do it?
21. What should be done?
22. How should it be done?
23. To what other uses could this be put?
24. In what other ways could this be used?

25. To what use could waste be put?
26. What can I make this look like?
27. What other process could be adapted to this job?
28. Out of whose book can I take a leaf? What leaf?
29. What changes can be made in the process or the way it works?
30. In what form could this be made?
31. How can we appeal more to the senses?
32. What about making it bigger? What can we add or multiply?
33. What if this were preposterously overstated? Exaggerated?
34. What if this were smaller? Omit. Divide. Minify. Lower. Less. Understate.
35. What can we substitute?
36. How can we make a game of it?
37. Can it be rearranged? The pattern changed? Cause and effect?
38. Vice-versa? Reverse the roles? Say it in reverse? Turn it around? The unexpected? Combination? Merged?
39. What is physically close to this?
40. What is this part of?
41. How would I like to see this thing come out? How else? How else?
42. How can this be made *vivid* hair? How can it be dramatized?
43. Discuss the problem with others.
44. What do I *not* know about the problem?

Often, this approach will help you find the new way to develop an execution or at least a new way to view the problem. Perhaps it will even generate the "big idea."

Finally, The Checklist

What makes a good advertisement or a good commercial? How can you evaluate it? How can you tell if it will work or if you need to do some more thinking? So far, we've covered the basics of translating an advertising strategy into an execution. We've made some specific suggestions on what to look for. We've learned what the experts say.

Now, here's a summary of how to judge an advertisement or a commercial. Here are eight checkpoints which will help you evaluate an execution. Of course, the first major question is "Is the advertisement or commercial on strategy?" In other words, does it translate the strategy that has been developed? If the answer to this question is "no," then go back and start over. If it's "yes," check the next seven points to see if it is a good ad.

1. Is the advertisement on strategy?
2. Is the ad written to a single person?
3. Is this ad single-minded? Does it try to sell just one thing or idea?
4. Does the message offer a benefit to the consumer?
5. Is the ad customer-oriented rather than company-oriented?

6. Have I controlled the execution so it doesn't overwhelm the message?
7. Have I told the whole story I want to tell? Have I avoided assuming the audience knows more than they do?
8. Does the advertisement ask for the order?

If you can answer yes, to all these checkpoints, you're on the road to maximizing the advertising investment. You've translated your advertising strategy and created a strong selling message. In short, you probably have a solid advertising execution.

Chapter 9
Creative Guidelines for Media

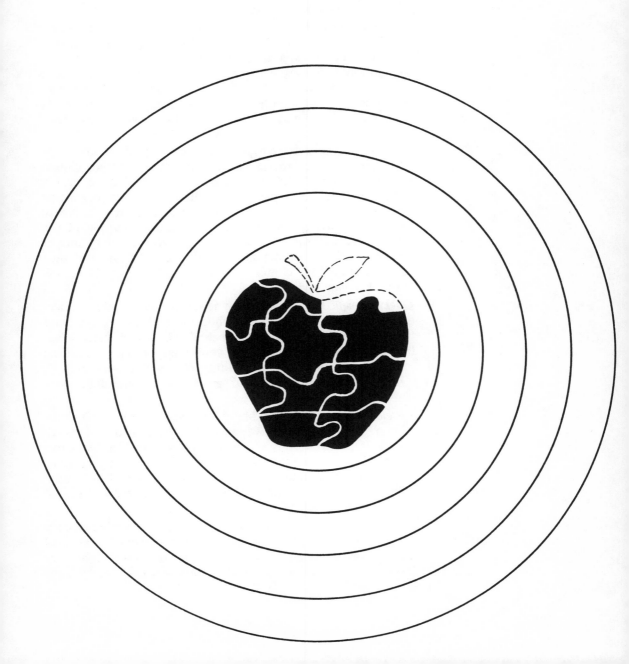

After our in-depth discussions of advertising strategy and execution, you probably are asking, "Should different creative executions be used for messages placed in different media?" The answer is yes. Each medium has its own advantages and limitations.

Because each medium has a direct influence on the possible and potential execution of the advertising message, we will review them separately. The lists are not inclusive, but they point out the major factors to consider when developing an advertising execution for each media vehicle.

Newspapers

Newspapers are essentially a non-selective medium. That is, many types of people buy newspapers. They may or may not have an interest in your product. To be effective, a newspaper advertising execution must:

1. *Gain Immediate Attention.* Most newspaper readers are "scanners" rather than "readers." They skim through the newspaper seeking articles or advertising of immediate interest. Most people don't look through a newspaper twice, so your ad only has a one-time opportunity. Therefore, your advertisement must attract immediate attention. It must attract your prospects quickly and thoroughly. It must say "This ad is for you. Read it."

2. *Rise Above Clutter.* Newspapers are filled with ads shouting for attention. Often there are several ads on each page. Unless you're able to purchase an entire page to yourself, there's going to be competition, usually called "clutter." To overcome this "clutter," your advertisement must be clear, concise and easy to read. It must be able to compete for the attention of the reader against all the other ads. Even if placed at the bottom of the page, with many other ads stacked on top of it, your ad must be seen among the "clutter." It must literally shout "Hey, look at me. I'm worth your time."

3. *Offer a Benefit.* Because so much newspaper advertising is price-oriented, your advertisement must immediately make your benefit clear. When you're competing with a bold, black headline that says "50% Off," and you're not offering a reduced price, the benefit or problem solution of your execution must be clear. A strong benefit-laden ad can often overcome all the price competition.

4. *Develop a Distinctive Look.* Many retail stores seek to develop a certain "look" in their newspaper advertising, usually through layout. Because there is so much competition, if a distinctive approach can be developed, it helps set the advertising apart. Customers come to know and recognize the style of the advertising. This helps in the sorting out process, particularly for those who are scanning the pages.

5. *Set the Mood of the Advertiser.* In addition to a distinctive look for recognition, the way a newspaper advertisement is executed often gives the impression of the type of store. Light, airy layouts indicate fashion or more expensive goods. Heavy black

numbers and illustrations say bargain, low price, savings. The "mood" of the advertisement, particularly for a retail outlet, often helps pre-select the audience to whom the advertising will appeal.

6. *Be Readable.* While you might think that pictures run upside down, sideways, or with words missing might attract attention, it just isn't so. People scan newspapers. They won't and usually don't take the time to figure out what you're trying to do with a clever layout, headline, or other form of execution. Other things are more important. Strive for readability in your execution. Make it easy for your prospect to know what benefit you offer or what problem your product will solve. Don't play games.

7. *Say "Buy Now" — Tomorrow May Be Too Late.* Newspapers are time-oriented. There will be another one out tonight or tomorrow. For that reason, your execution must be oriented to immediate action. Do everything you can to help the prospect decide to buy now. Give full details. Answer all questions. Tell everything the prospect needs to know. And, be sure to ask for the order.

Magazines

While magazines are another form of print advertising, they are very different from newspapers. Magazines are becoming more and more selective in their audiences. Once the mass audience magazines dominated, but now the big trend is toward more highly specialized publications. This means readers know the subject of the magazine and are interested in it. This "selectivity" means there are some definite differences between advertising executions for magazines and newspapers.

1. *Be More Direct.* Because the audience is usually pre-selected by the magazine's editorial content, appeals can be more direct. There's no need to select the audience, they're already there. For example, most readers of *Sports Illustrated* know and understand sports. It's not necessary to explain soccer to this audience but you might have to in a newspaper ad. In a magazine you can go directly to the benefit and get right to the point. Be more specific. The interest is already there. It's up to your execution to make the most of it.

2. *Longer Reading Time.* While newspapers are usually scanned, magazines are often read and re-read. Because magazines are used in a more leisurely fashion, more time is available to fully develop your sales message. People will read longer copy in magazines. They're more inclined to compare charts, follow diagrams, read directions and comparisons. Look at magazines as already having an interested audience to whom you can explain things.

3. *Readers Want More Information.* While your execution should tell the whole story, the use of coupons, free offers, booklets and other methods of providing more information are especially good in magazine advertisements. Take full advantage of this

opportunity to fill in the blanks in your execution with additional details to be sent to interested readers.

4. *Color and Reproduction.* Magazines offer the major advantage of color and reproduction of your execution. Newspapers are often limited to black and white. Magazines give you a rainbow of color plus excellent reproduction. This advantage allows you to illustrate small details, to blow-up photographs, and to use the appetite appeal of color or exact replicas of the product for identification purposes in retail outlets. Use the advantage of magazine color and reproduction in your executions.

5. *Greater Competition.* Because your audience is pre-selected, direct competition from other advertisers is usually greater in a magazine. For example, in *House Beautiful*, you may find 10 to 15 advertisers of dining room furniture, all in full color, all in your approximate price range. With this added competition, it's vital that the benefit or problem solution of your execution be seen at a glance. While this competition may create some problems, it should be an opportunity for you. A great strategy and a strong execution will stand out even more in the face of competition. You quickly become the *one* product the consumer wants because your advantage is obvious.

Business Publications

Advertising in business publications, unlike most consumer newspapers and magazines, is designed to do a different job, usually to generate leads for the field sales force. Therefore, your execution in business publications is usually a bit different from consumer advertising. Most products and services advertised in business publications are quite specialized. More emphasis is put on details and specifics than is found in consumer advertising.

There are two primary types of business publications, vertical and horizontal. Horizontal publications deal with a specific job function, as in *Sales & Marketing Management.* Whether a person is a sales manager for an auto dealership or a steel company, the problems are the same — hiring sales people, motivating them, controlling expenses, payroll, etc.

A vertical publication, on the other hand, such as *Advertising Age*, deals with an industry at all levels. Whether your interest is creative, media, account work, budgeting of advertising, etc., you'll find news and information of interest.

The type of publication makes a difference in your execution. The specific things to do in business publications are:

1. *Be Factual.* Business publication readers are interested in facts. There can be little hint of exaggeration or generalization. Readers want details and they want information they can use. Tell how, why, when and where your product should be used.

2. *Rational Appeals Are Best.* The business reader usually is interested in making an evaluative judgment between several products. Therefore, rational appeals of an economic or business nature are best. There is little room for flamboyance in business publication executions. Emotional appeals also may fall flat

unless they are supported with sound economic reasons to buy.

3. *Case Histories Are Excellent.* Visual or laboratory proof of performance works well. Readers can compare the experience of competitors or people in similar businesses with your product or service. They can then judge whether or not the product would work for them. Proof of claims, backed by case histories, usually provides the evidence necessary to show the benefit or provide the solution to a problem.

4. *Deal in Specifics.* Glowing generalities don't work in business advertising executions. Be specific. Explaining how or why this product provides this benefit always strengthens the sales message.

5. *Personalize to a Particular Job or Business.* Business publication readers are involved with their own particular problems or situations. It is usually best to personalize the appeal and the benefit in your execution to a specific area of interest. If necessary, use more than one execution to tell several benefits. Be sure the execution you develop is direct and to the point.

6. *Speak the Language.* Don't try to speak the language of the industry unless you know it. Slang, used incorrectly, immediately identifies you as an outsider, one who probably doesn't know the business and, therefore, doesn't understand the problem to be solved. If there's a question, get someone who knows the field to look over the words. One of the greatest sins in a business publication execution is not speaking the language correctly.

Direct Mail/Direct Sales

Direct mail/direct sales is unique among the various advertising media discussed in this chapter. It is the one time where a single execution must do the entire selling job.

The difference between direct mail and direct sales is primarily the medium in which the message appears. Direct mail refers to items delivered through the postal service to the prospect's home. Direct sales means the product goes directly from the manufacturer or advertiser to the consumer without a middleman. Both, however, have similar requirements for effective advertising executions.

1. *Get Attention/Get It Opened.* A direct sales execution has only one opportunity to make a sale. That's right now. If the direct mail envelope isn't opened or the direct sales message ignored, the advertising has failed. It's the primary job of the execution to get the attention of the prospect and get him involved immediately.

2. *Tell All.* The direct advertising execution must tell all the prospect needs to know to make a decision. There is no place for shopping, comparing or evaluating. The direct advertiser must include all the benefits and information necessary for a decision. That includes price, sizes, shapes, colors, ordering information, etc.

3. *Overcome Dislike.* Many people have strong feelings about "junk

111

mail'' or direct offers. The execution of the direct sales message must overcome these feelings. The best way is to show the benefit or problem solution immediately. That way the message will be read in its entirety or at least enough so that the benefit is clear.

4. *Support the Price Asked.* There is no chance for physical comparison in direct advertising. The execution must immediately support the price asked. This can be done in several ways, by problem solving, by building up benefits, by strong appeals to consumer wants, etc.

5. *Be Direct, Don't Waste Words.* There's no room for wasted words in a direct sales execution. Everything must be aimed at taking the consumer through the story in the least possible time so that a favorable decision is reached.

6. *Make An Offer.* What is being offered, the price, and how to obtain it must be clear at a glance. Be sure the prospect knows what you have for sale and how to get it.

7. *Ask for Action.* Everything in direct sales must be headed in one direction, toward the request for action. If no request is made, the details are not clear, the action not specified, then the best advertising in the world has gone for naught. Direct sales advertising is action-oriented. Be sure your message leads directly to the offer, and then ask for the purchase.

Outdoor and Transit

Outdoor and transit are among the most powerful advertising media, but many people find them difficult to work in. The reason is the lack of time and space for the message.

Outdoor could refer to any type of outdoor sign. Here it is restricted to outdoor posters, painted signs, or spectacular displays that are more than locational or directional. Transit are the signs and posters appearing in or on public transportation such as buses, trains and subways. While this type of advertising has been involved in much controversy in the past few years, it remains a major form of advertising communication. Follow these steps for proper execution.

1. *Be Graphic and Visual.* In outdoor and transit ads, the visual idea is usually the basis for the message. Symbols are widely and effectively used. Graphics must be bright and bold so they can be seen and comprehended at a glance.

2. *Use Only One Sales Point.* Most outdoor posters must be seen and understood in 10 seconds or less. Therefore, it is vital that the message contain only one sales point. Be single-minded.

3. *Use Only Seven Words.* Studies have shown the average reader can see and comprehend a maximum of seven words and two graphic elements in the time he is exposed to an outdoor board. Keep it simple.

4. *Identify the Client and Product.* Don't assume the viewer knows

your product or your name. Particularly, don't assume he knows your claim. Make the name of the product, the advertiser, and the claim clear and prominent.

5. *Use Emotional Appeals.* Emotional appeals make the most memorable executions. Use them wherever possible.

In-Store and Promotional Materials

One of the most misunderstood areas of advertising is in-store and promotional advertising execution. Promotional materials are designed to gain consumer interest and involvement in such things as sweepstakes, contests, premiums, etc. In-store materials are used primarily at the point-of-purchase to induce a sale such as posters, signs, shelf-talkers, etc. Because they require different advertising executions, we must use a separate set of rules. The following suggestions differentiate in-store and promotional materials from other media forms.

1. *Get Attention.* Because in-store materials are the last thing a prospect sees before purchase, attention is vital. If the in-store material is not seen, all has gone for naught.

2. *Do Only One Job.* A major mistake with most in-store and promotional materials is trying to do too much. Stick to one sales message. If the idea is to promote a sweepstakes, do that. Subordinate the sales message for the product. If the idea is to get entries in a contest, concentrate the execution on that point. Do only one thing, but do it well.

3. *Make Brand Identification Clear.* The identification of the brand making the offer or the reason to buy must be clear. Don't allow the consumer to get confused about the brand. Make the brand an integral part of the execution.

4. *Be Direct.* Don't hide your benefit or problem solution in an in-store poster or a promotional piece. Be direct. Make the offer large enough to read at a glance. Make the benefit totally clear on the first reading.

5. *Include a Place for the Price on In-Store Materials.* Too many times the beauty of the materials becomes so overriding in an execution that the most important point to many consumers, the price, is forgotten. Include a place where the price can be included or written in by the retailer.

Radio

Radio is a medium unto itself. It requires the greatest of imagination, understanding, and empathy. Used correctly, radio can be one of the strongest methods of communicating a sales message. Used incorrectly, it can be one of the dullest. There is one cardinal rule in radio: Do not use it to read print advertisement over the air. That's a total misuse of the medium.

Radio is a unique medium. It can be extremely powerful if the following rules are followed.

1. *Write for the Ear and the Mind.* There are no pictures. Write for the ear and the mind. Draw on the imagination. Build images.

Ask people to involve themselves, to join you in their mind's eye.

2. *Intrude to Get Attention.* Radio is used primarily as a background medium. You must intrude to get attention. Break through the mental barrier which puts radio in the background. Get attention and once you've gotten attention, hold it.

3. *Entertain, but Sell.* Audiences come to radio to be entertained. Your execution must entertain also. Never forget the purpose of radio advertising is to deliver a sales message. Entertain, but sell. Don't let the execution overwhelm the message.

4. *Make One Sales Point.* One sales message, well made, is best for radio. Don't try to cram too many sales ideas into a commercial. You will only succeed in getting nothing across. Make only one sales message but be sure it is a benefit, or the solution to a consumer problem.

5. *Keep It Simple.* People can't see the product or what you are doing, so keep the message simple. Make it clear and direct. Invite participation. That helps simplify complex ideas.

6. *You can't repeat the Brand Name or the Sales Point Too Often.* Think how many times it's necessary to repeat a telephone number until you can remember it. It's the same with radio. Repeat the brand and the sales point so often it becomes redundant.

7. *Make Ad Sound Like People Talk.* Radio is verbal communication. It should be written the way people talk. It doesn't have to be in complete sentences, but it must be in complete thoughts. Does it sound like you're talking to someone or trying to sell them something? Talking is always best.

8. *Use the Classic Radio Writing Formula.* There is a formula for writing a radio commercial. It goes like this:

>   1. Tell them what you're going to tell them.
>   2. Tell them.
>   3. Tell them what you've told them.

Use this formula. It works.

Television

There are more suggestions and ideas on how to write television commercials than any other form of communication. Apparently, not all of them work or there wouldn't be so many dull commercials on the air. Here are some of the best suggestions on how to use this most powerful advertising medium.

1. *Make sure the Commercial is Visual.* Perhaps the most important, yet most misunderstood fact is that television is basically a visual medium. The pictures are the most important part. The words merely support the pictures. A good way to judge a television commercial's effectiveness is to turn off the sound. Now, see if you can get the message. If the commercial is a good execution, you should be able to understand the message without the words.

2. *Demonstrate.* Television is a demonstration medium. Show your product in action. Show how it works. Show what it can do. Demonstrate the benefit if at all possible.

3. *Be Intrusive.* Like radio, people do not come to television to see and hear the commercials. You must be intrusive. You must get attention. You must break through the barrier of disinterest.

4. *Make Only One Sales Point.* A good television message is not how many selling points you can cram into a 30-second period. It's how effectively you can make one sales point in 30 seconds. There's a world of difference in that one concept. Make one sales point and make it clearly and completely.

5. *Achieve Clear Brand Identification.* Too often, the brand in a television commercial is lost or confused by the consumer. Be sure the brand appears strongly in the spot. Achieving brand recognition is second only to the clear understanding of the primary sales message.

6. *Don't Let the Idea Overpower the Message.* Don't get so involved in the demonstration or the visual effects that the product is lost. The primary idea is to communicate a sales message. Entertain but don't entertain to the exclusion of your sales message.

7. *Remember People Interpret Television Literally.* While radio often relies on the imagination, television is a very literal medium. What people see is what they believe. Be sure your demonstrations and examples are correct and honest.

8. *Make the Television Commercial Like a Drama.* Like the classic drama, your commercial should have a beginning, a middle and an end. Be sure your message is complete.

The preceding pages have given you a brief overview of the primary points to keep in mind when translating a strategy into an execution for the various media. Certainly these are not all the points which should be considered, but they are the major ones from an evaluation standpoint. They are sound advice for writers of advertisements and commercials. While each medium has certain strengths and weaknesses, there is a common thread that runs through all of them.

1. Be sure the benefit or problem solution comes through clearly.

2. Make one major sales point and make it clearly.

3. Make sure the brand is clearly identified.

4. Keep your message simple but be sure it is complete.

These four rules apply to all forms of media and all forms of advertising. If you use them to evaluate your proposed advertising and it scores highly on all four, you have a good chance of success.

Appendix

Restrictions and Regulations on the Creative Product

During the past several years, regulations and restrictions that affect what can and can't be said in advertising have increased enormously. Consumer groups, government, and the industry itself have become more and more involved.

In the past, advertising was usually judged on whether it was "false or misleading," but now it is being questioned whether or not some advertising should even be allowed in front of certain audiences. Where previous restrictions were on advertising that was obviously false, increasing attention is being given to advertising which could conceivably mislead consumers or in which all the facts are not presented. Questions have even arisen about the efficacy of persuasive messages in the marketplace.

In this section, we will take a brief look at the groups which regulate or restrict advertising. In addition, we will review some of the general areas that are in question or that seem to cause the most trouble for advertisers.

To illustrate what could conceivably happen if restrictions and regulations go too far, we have reprinted an article by Don R. Cunningham, former senior vice president, at Foote, Cone & Belding advertising agency. While Cunningham's comments are somewhat "tongue-in-cheek," his fears about the over-regulation of advertising is a very real one. The words were written in 1971 but they are just as current today as they were then. More and more restrictions have been put on what can and can't be said in advertising. We seem to be rapidly approaching what Cunningham called the "Orwellian Vision of Advertising."

Orwellian Visions of Advertising/ *By Don R. Cunningham*

Pictured to the right is a bill-board in 1984

You don't see anything, right? Right!

Picture a TV commercial for a Suzuki motorcycle. The ad opens on a still slide of the new GT-2000. (Action shots are not possible since such photographs tend to distort the machine and may glamorize the motorcycle.)

The announcer says:

"This is a motorcycle. It is one of the 42 brands available in the United States. All are about equal in performance and value.

"This one is called Suzuki. It's a little more expensive than most. However, the International Research Consortium has confirmed it performs up to 7.3 per cent better than most — when subjected to a conscientiously applied program of careful driving and regular professional care.

"Some people enjoy riding motorcycles. However, other people don't.

"What's more, the Federal Trade Commission warns that motorcycling may be injurious to your health. Motorcycles are noisy, they pollute, tear up the soil, encourage motorcycle gangs, and may contribute to the delinquency of minors.

"In the unlikely event that you're interested in one, call this toll free number, which the FCC advises us to tell you is not really toll free."

(Super number and disclaimer.)

Now visualize a beautiful full-color magazine ad showing a delicious Sunkist orange. The ad says:

"Sprayed with pesticides. Quality may vary due to climate and seasonal differences. Excessive amounts of vitamin C have an indeterminate effect on personal health."

The fairness doctrine is noble in intent. But if both sides of all controversial subjects should be aired, we'll find nearly everything can be controversial. For example, a noted forester recently commented that a little fire every now and then clears out underbrush, makes the forest more healthy, and can be ecologically valuable.

So here's a radio commercial from the Anti-Forest-Fire Prevention League:

"Don't believe that stupid bear. A little forest fire can be fun. Help keep America brown."

Jingle: Only You Can Start a Forest Fire.

Or with the legalization of pot:

"Kids — Come fly with me. Consult your nearest pusher. You'll find him listed in the Yellow Pages."

There are some other developments in advertising.

Since postal rates are now averaging $1 per copy for magazines, circulation is much smaller and entirely through newsstands. Newspapers are phasing out. Not enough advertising to meet the ever-increasing costs. Facsimile is taking over without advertising. Each of the 72 TV channels accepting advertising now gags commercials. Fifteen seconds is the standard length. No commercial may be used more than five times.

It's 1984. We have laws that tell us not only what we may say in advertising but what may be advertised, which media may be used, and to whom we may advertise. That's why we have no more outdoor. Our copy presents facts. With no emotional appeals. Children are shielded from advertising.

The list of taboo product categories has grown from cigarets to all drug items (pills can't solve all problems), cosmetics (they conjure up false hopes), and fashions (whoever looks like the fashion model). If you think this can't happen here, think again. It is happening. Now.

Please understand: Many of the changes taking place are due to failings within the advertising industry. The "permissible lie" is no basis for business morality. Also understand that not all the changes taking place are necessarily bad. But more good things will happen to advertising — and to the public and to the economy — if we ourselves help shape the future.

At this very moment legislation is shaping advertising. Consumer groups are shaping advertising. Young people and their teachers are shaping advertising. What are you doing to shape advertising? You can do nothing. You can complain. Or you can act . . ."[1]

Who Regulates Advertising?

Granted, Cunningham's comments may be biased. But, with pending legislation, some of the visions he had of what might happen in 1984 might just occur.

Currently, four groups have direct control over what can and can't be said or is or isn't said in advertising. These are:

1. The advertiser.
2. The government.
3. Industry groups.
4. Public groups and organizations.

Let's discuss each group separately.

1. *The Advertiser.* The strongest regulatory force over advertising is probably the advertiser himself. Most advertisers are honest businessmen who are interested in the longterm. It is to their advantage to be honest and fair in their advertising because advertising builds their businesses. They know if their advertising is false or they mislead the consumer, repeat purchases won't take place. Many advertisers have established a set or code of advertising rules, what can and can't be said or done in their advertising. They use these rules not only to guide their own people but their outside suppliers and advertising agencies as well. The strongest restriction on advertising is always imposed by the person who runs the ad.

2. *The Government.* All levels of government — federal, state and local — now control or restrict advertising to some extent. *Federal.* Most federal regulations are developed and enforced by governmental agencies such as the Federal Trade Commission, the Food & Drug Administration, Federal Communications Commission, U. S. Department of Agriculture, etc. When it comes to advertising, each has its own area of interest. Most federal regulations have the basic purpose of preventing false or misleading advertising, labeling, identification of contents, or other activities which might be harmful to consumers. These regulations are enforced through such remedies as "cease and desist orders," injunctions and even seizure orders.

The primary force in federal regulation is the

Federal Trade Commission which enforces the "false and misleading" doctrine primarily against advertisers who are engaged in interstate commerce. They publish a set of guidelines and develop rulings which they use as a basis for enforcement. Advertisers use interpretations of these rulings as a basis to avoid legal problems. The FTC is becoming much more active in investigation of advertising complaints and the developing of trade regulation rulings.

Another major group regulating advertising is the Food & Drug Administration. Their primary involvement is in labeling and packaging. They publish rules and guidelines which advertisers follow, particularly in the area of labeling.

Another group which has some influence over advertising is the Federal Communications Commission. This agency licenses all radio and television stations in the country. Because they can withhold approval to broadcast, they indirectly affect advertising on the airwaves.

The U. S. Department of Agriculture, Postal Service and other agencies also have various rules and regulations which directly affect advertising. Since regulations and rulings change so rapidly, advertisers are constantly monitoring the latest rulings and regulations developed by all federal agencies.

State. Some states have laws or regulations which affect advertisers and advertising. For example, some types of consumer promotions are illegal in certain states. Wisconsin has strong regulations concerning the legality of advertiser-sponsored sweepstakes and contests. Some states have restrictions on various types of media such as outdoor advertising in Maine. Other states, such as Florida, have developed strong restrictions on advertising offers using the word "free" or other promotional activities. Probably the most common state laws deal with the advertising of alcoholic beverages. Each advertiser must locate and follow the various state restrictions on his own product.

Local. Some cities and towns have developed their own local laws which restrict or regulate advertising. The most common is probably the regulation concerning "going out of business" sales. Some localities have set specific time limits, licensing arrangements, or other restrictions on advertising and the advertiser who is "going out of business." Most restrictions deal with how the advertising may appear and the length of time it may be run. Another common restriction is on "bait and switch" advertising. Other localities have restrictions on such things as real estate, forms of entertainment, alcoholic beverages, and others. Again, advertisers must respect these laws and it is their responsibility to learn about them.

3. *Industry Groups.* Advertisers, agencies and media have long

sought to regulate themselves through industry codes or agreements rather than have governmental help. The argument has been made that the advertisers know best how to develop these regulations and what restrictions and regulations should be set. For the most part, this approach has been fairly successful in the past. There is increasing evidence, however, that this approach is losing out to formal regulation. Several industry groups have been organized to set advertising regulations. The most well recognized are:

National Advertising Review Board. This is a national group consisting of 30 advertisers, 10 advertising agencies, and 10 persons not involved in advertising. The group is part of the National Advertising Division of the Better Business Bureau. Its primary function is to investigate and arbitrate questionable advertising among national advertisers. NARB becomes involved in questions of ethics, good taste, and even squabbles among advertisers about competitive or comparative advertising. The group has grown in stature during the past few years and is considered the "court of last authority" in the field of self-regulation.

Better Business Bureaus. This organization polices advertising on the local level. This group hears consumer complaints about false or misleading advertising appearing in local media. For the most part, it is concerned with retail advertising. In addition to following up on complaints, it also investigates advertising practices on its own and issues complaints against offenders. While each BBB is local, it is usually a member of a national organization which gives it greater power.

National Association of Broadcasters. The prime regulatory force in radio and television advertising is the NAB code. The code is developed by broadcasters, advertisers, and advertising agencies and is generally followed by all these groups, whether or not they are NAB members. The NAB code covers all types of broadcast advertising, from what type of commercials may be accepted to the method by which the advertising is presented to children. The NAB code, while not binding, is usually followed by both national and local advertisers and stations.

Trade Associations. Many trade associations, such as those groups representing the candy, meat, and liquor industries, have developed sets of rules and regulations concerning advertising by their members. Most of these regulations are designed to promote the industry and prevent unscrupulous advertisers from unfairly presenting or representing their products. While regulations of this type are usually developed for self-preservation, often they are accepted by other groups.

Networks, Newspapers, Stations and Individual Media. Various media also have regulations and restrictions on advertising, usually concerning what they will and won't accept. Networks, for example, screen all commercials sent them. Through a censoring group, they determine if the advertising is acceptable in terms of its presentation, content, ability to mislead, etc. Those which fail to pass are not accepted for broadcast or are returned to the advertiser with suggestions for revision.

Local stations also make the same decisions on spot or local advertising. Both networks and local stations use the NAB code as a basis for decision. Many newspapers and magazines also have a code of advertising acceptability which they use to screen advertising. For example, *Good Housekeeping* and *Parent's Magazine* require proof of performance by various products before they will accept the advertising. The *New York Times* has developed restrictions on the size and content of X-rated movie advertising.

Other media have similar restrictions and regulations, much of which is based on obscenity, local regulations, or the owner's own prerogatives.

4. *Public Groups and Organizations.* Civic, public and consumer groups have a certain amount of control over advertising through their criticism to advertisers. For example, the consumer group Action for Children's Television (ACT), has been quite successful in influencing the type and content of advertising directed to children.

Other consumer groups, through letter-writing campaigns, protest meetings, etc., have caused major changes in the advertising of various products. Most advertisers, because they recognize the power of consumer groups, are anxious to work with them to develop acceptable advertising.

With exceptions, most controls over advertising are voluntary. The major exception is the regulation of "false and misleading advertising." Many consumers don't understand how self-regulation works and, as a result, are continuously calling for more federal and state regulations. While some forms of regulation are undoubtedly needed, most advertisers will follow the rules which have been set up. Those who don't soon find the lack of repeat customers drives them out of business anyway. In the past, the government has been content to let advertisers regulate themselves; however, there are many more controls today than there were a few years ago and there will probably be more in the future.

Regulatory Differences Between Print and Broadcast

One advertising regulation that is often misunderstood is that what can appear in print sometimes can't appear in broadcast. Most print media are privately owned and, thus, not licensed or restricted. Publishers claim immunity to control under the First Amendment's Freedom of Speech rule.

On the other hand, all radio and television stations are licensed by the federal government. There is, therefore, greater control over what can be done and said in broadcast than in print, even though it is often implied rather than actually written. For example, while beer and wine can be advertised in broadcast, with certain restrictions, the NAB code prohibits any advertising of hard liquor. Print media, on the other hand, can accept advertising for all types of alcoholic beverages if government regulations are followed. Cigarette advertising is also prohibited from broadcast advertising. Other products such as X-rated movies, birth control devices, etc., are restricted in broadcast because their ads could be considered in bad taste. Print media, however, may accept these types of advertising, unless they are considered "obscene" by the publisher.

So don't forget that there is a major difference between the regulations for print and broadcast.

The Basic Areas of Regulation

Because rules and regulations concerning advertising content vary so widely and change so rapidly, the best recommendation for determining the acceptability of certain ideas or executions is a good legal counsel.

Many advertising claims fall into the general area known as "puffery." This simply means that an advertiser has a right to make certain opinion claims of quality or preference for his product with no actual support. In addition, certain claims which are so obvious as to need no support can also be considered "puffing."

There is a fine line, however, between "puffery" and distortion of the truth. Legal counsel is often needed to determine the difference. All advertising for major national advertisers usually must be approved by their legal departments. While this solves many problems in advance, many advertising people argue it stifles creativity.

There are certain areas that affect advertisers regardless of the type of product advertised or the scope of the sales operation. The major areas of concern are:

1. *Rights of Privacy.* Advertisers cannot use the names, pictures, or likenesses of people for advertising purposes without written permission. This same regulation also extends in certain cases to buildings, organizations, corporations, and other well-known or unique articles.

2. *Deception of the Average Person.* Most advertising claims are judged on the basis of whether or not the claim would "deceive or mislead the average person." The fact that the advertising can be interpreted by a knowledgeable person makes no difference. It is this "average person" rule which is the yardstick. In addition, actual deception is not necessary. The test is whether or not the advertising has the "capacity" or "tendency" to deceive. This is a very difficult area in which to make judgments.

3. *Demonstrations.* Demonstrations of products must be totally clear and honest and not have the capacity to deceive. Support for a claim must be provided if the demonstration takes place in a laboratory or with a test group of people. There are certain limitations on all demonstrations, especially those made using a mock-up or a simulation. Usually, a disclaimer must appear with the advertisement explaining the situation under which the demonstration took place.

4. *Comparative Advertising.* Detracting or belittling the product or

service of a competitor is not allowed. It can be considered an unfair method of competition and may even generate a claim of libel.

5.   *Testimonials.* Advertisers cannot make any claims in a testimonial which they could not make in a regular advertisement. In addition, the person making the testimonial must be competent to make the statement attributed to them.

6.   *Contests and Sweepstakes.* Contests and sweepstakes are legal as long as they don't become lotteries. A lottery has three elements — prize, chance, and consideration. As long as all three aren't present, the promotion is usually legal. There also are restrictions on the awarding of prizes.

7.   *Copyrights and Trademarks.* Extensive use of materials which have been copyrighted cannot be used without the permission of the copyright holder. A trademark is any word, name, symbol, device, or combination of these used to identify a manufacturer's products or services. These elements or names cannot be used in any illegal way. They usually require permission of the trademark holder for use in advertising.

8.   *Flags and Money.* The U. S. flag or that of most foreign countries cannot be used in advertising. Incidental use as part of a scene or similar use is permissable. Generally, coins can be reproduced for advertising purposes but paper money cannot.[2]

Again, the above rules and regulations are quite general. They do, however, indicate areas where many advertising problems occur. Regardless of the situation, most creative executions should be cleared with a legal counsel.

Words That Attract Attention

Certain advertising words attract attention — legal attention, that is. They also are common words widely used in advertising executions. Some of these words — "red flag" words — seem to invite legal attention. Some of the more common are:

Free. If "free" is used as part of an offer, any and all conditions must be spelled out in close proximity to the physical use of the word.

New. The FTC has ruled that a product is no longer "new" after six months unless part of that time has been in an established test market.

Guarantee. Any guarantee must contain all terms and conditions under which the guarantee is offered.

Stop, End, Rid. These words are considered to be complete. An advertisement claiming to "stop" pimples must do so forever. The same goes for "end" and "rid." Usually no product can make this sort of claim.

Cure or Remedy. Great care must be taken with any product that claims to "cure" a problem or disease because it must do so completely. A cure is considered to remove the problem forever. The product must be able to support this point.

Doctors, White Coats, and Laboratories. Persons may not impersonate a doctor, dentist, nurse, or other medical person. Laboratories must be actual and laboratory results supported with actual tests.

Proof or Evidence. When proof or evidence is offered in support of an advertising claim, it must be from a recognized authority or based on tests conducted under scientific conditions.

Safe or Harmless. Two dangerous words. When used, they must spell out all conditions under which the product is safe or harmless and conditions which may cause problems.

A Final Word

One of the most misunderstood restrictions on advertising is the subject of total content. This simply means that each and every sentence in an advertisement may be factually true. You can support each sentence taken separately. Put together, though, the sentences may form another meaning. In other words, while each sentence is true, the total content of the advertisement or commercial may tend to deceive or mislead. In this case, the advertiser is liable. This is the area of intent. Did the advertiser mean to mislead? Was the ad intended to deceive? That is the judgment which the law will make. Therefore, the best way to view an advertisement or commercial is not just whether each sentence is correct but whether or not the overall intent of the advertising is correct. Advertisers have a right to persuade. They do not have a right to deceive.

While some advertising people believe legal counsel is primarily interested in preventing or destroying great advertising ideas, that usually is not the case. The truth is the laws relating to advertising are so complex that what may be ok today is out tomorrow. The best way to handle legal problems is to learn the rules, stay within the rules, and sell within the rules.

Notes

Chapter 2

1. Schramm, Wilbur, and Donald F. Roberts, *The Process and Effects of Mass Communications* (Urbana, IL: University of Illinois Press, 1954).

2. Kotler, Philip, "Behavioral Models for Analyzing Buyers," *Journal of Marketing*, Vol. 29 (October, 1965), pp. 37-45.

3. Rogers, Everett M., and F. Floyd Schoemaker, *Communication of Innovations*, 2nd Ed. (New York: The Free Press, 1971).

4. Schultz, Don E., and Dennis G. Martin, *Strategic Advertising Campaigns* (Chicago: Crain Books, division of Crain Communications, Inc., 1980).

5. Krugman, Herbert, "The Impact of Television: Learning Without Involvement," *Public Opinion Quarterly* (Fall, 1965), pp. 349-356.

6. Lavidge, Robert J., and Gary A. Steiner, "A Model for Predicting Measurements of Advertising Effectiveness," *Journal of Marketing* (October, 1961), pp. 59-62.

Chapter 3

1. McCarthy, E. Jerome, *Basic Marketing: A Managerial Approach*, Fifth Edition (Homewood, IL: Richard D. Irwin, Inc., 1975)

2. Schultz, Don E., and Dennis G. Martin, *Strategic Advertising Campaigns*, (Chicago: Crain Books, division of Crain Communications, Inc., 1980).

Chapter 4

1. Adams, James R., *Sparks Off My Anvil: From 30 Years in Advertising* (New York: Harper & Row, 1958).

2. Ibid.

Chapter 5

1. Reeves, Rosser, *Reality in Advertising* (New York: Knopf, 1961).

2. Ogilvy, David, *Confessions of an Advertising Man* (New York: Ballantine Books, 1963).

3. Trout, Jack, and Al Ries, *Positioning "Positioning"* (Chicago: Crain Books, division of Crain Communications, Inc., 1972).

Chapter 6

1. Aaker, David A., and John G. Myers. *Advertising Management* (Englewood Cliffs, N.J.: Prentice-Hall, 1975).

Chapter 7

1. Young, James Webb, *A Technique for Producing Ideas* (Chicago: Crain Books, division of Crain Communications, Inc., 1960).

Chapter 8

1. Bernbach, William, by permission.

2. From "Communications of an Advertising Man: Selections from the Speeches, Articles, Memoranda and Miscellaneous Writings of Leo Burnett." Copyright 1961 by Leo Burnett Company, Inc. For Private Distribution Only. Used with permission.

3. Cone, Fairfax M., *The Blue Streak: Some Observations, Mostly About Advertising* (Chicago: Crain Books, division of Crain Communications, Inc., 1975).

4. Ogilvy, David *Confessions of an Advertising Man.* (New York: Ballantine Books, 1963).

5. Brower, Charles, *Me and Other Advertising Geniuses.* (Garden City, N.Y.: Doubleday, 1974).

Appendix

1. Cunningham, Don R., *Broadcasting*, October 25, 1971.

2. Hackett, Byron, *How to Keep Your Ads Out of Court* (New York: J. Walter Thompson Company, undated).

Picture Credits

All ads, photos, and storyboards reprinted with permission.

FIGURE 1-1—Source:
Procter & Gamble Co.
Agency: Benton & Bowles.

FIGURE 1-2—Source:
Colgate Palmolive Co.
Agency: Ted Bates & Co.

FIGURE 1-3—Source:
Benton & Bowles.

FIGURE 4-1—Source:
Procter & Gamble Co.

FIGURE 4-2—Source:
Procter & Gamble Co.
Agency: Grey Advertising.

FIGURE 4-3—Source:
Procter & Gamble Co.
Agency: Leo Burnett U.S.A.

FIGURE 5-1—Source:
Polaroid Corp.
Agency: Doyle Dane Bernbach Inc.

FIGURE 5-2—Source:
Ralston Purina Co.

FIGURE 5-3—Source:
Mobil Corp.
Agency: Doyle Dane Bernbach Inc.

FIGURE 5-4—Source:
Merrill Lynch,
Pierce, Fenner & Smith Inc.
Agency: Ogilvy & Mather.

FIGURE 5-5—Source:
Pepperidge Farm Inc.
Agency: Ogilvy & Mather.

FIGURE 5-6—Source:
Philip Morris U.S.A.
Agency: Leo Burnett U.S.A.

FIGURE 5-7—Source:
Kellogg Co.
Agency: Leo Burnett U.S.A.

FIGURE 5-8—Source:
Green Giant Co.
Agency: Leo Burnett U.S.A.

FIGURE 5-9—Source:
Seven-Up Co.

FIGURE 5-10—Source:
Anheuser-Busch Inc.
Agency: D'Arcy-MacManus & Masius Inc.

FIGURE 5-11—Source:
J. C. Penney Co.

FIGURE 5-12—Source:
Revlon Inc. © 1978.

FIGURE 5-13—Source:
General Foods Corp.
Agency: Grey Advertising Inc.

FIGURE 6-1—Source:
North Texas Commission.
Agency: Tracy-Locke.

FIGURE 6-2—Source:
Frito-Lay Inc. © 1978.
DORITOS ® is a registered trademark
of Frito-Lay Inc.
Agency: Tracy-Locke.

FIGURE 6-3—Source:
Dr. Pepper Co.
Agency: Young & Rubicam, New York.

FIGURE 6-4—(Reprinted with permission
of copyright owner, Clairol Inc.
All rights reserved.)

FIGURE 6-5—Source:
Philip Morris U.S.A.
Agency: Leo Burnett U.S.A.

FIGURE 6-6—Source:
Calvert Distillers Co.
Agency: Doyle Dane Bernbach Inc.

FIGURE 7-1—Source:
Sears, Roebuck & Co.
Agency: Foote, Cone & Belding Inc.

FIGURE 7-2—Source:
American Express Co.
Agency: Ogilvy & Mather Inc.

FIGURE 7-3—Source:
American Tourister Inc.
Agency: Doyle Dane Bernbach Inc.

FIGURE 7-4—Source:
Xerox Corp.
Agency: Needham, Harper & Steers Inc.

FIGURE 7-5—Source:
The Maytag Co.
Agency: Leo Burnett U.S.A.

FIGURE 7-6—Source:
Dannon Yogurt.
Agency: Marsteller Inc.

FIGURE 7-7—Source:
Courtesy of Miller Brewing Co.
Agency: McCann-Erickson Inc.

FIGURE 7-8—Source:
Leeming Division of Pfizer.
Agency: Ted Bates & Co. Inc.

FIGURE 7-9—Source:
General Foods Inc.
Agency: Grey Advertising Inc.

FIGURE 7-10—Source:
Volkswagen of America Inc.
Agency: Doyle Dane Bernbach Inc.